MARKET RESEARCH MADE EASY

Don Doman
Dell Dennison
Margaret Doman

Viva Books

New Delhi | Mumbai | Chennai | Kolkata | Bangalore | Hyderabad | Kochi

First Indian Edition 2006
Reprinted 2008

VIVA BOOKS PRIVATE LIMITED

- 4737/23 Ansari Road, Daryaganj, New Delhi 110 002
  E-mail: vivadelhi@vivagroupindia.net, Tel. 42242200
- Plot No. 76, Service Industries, Shirvane, Sector 1, Nerul, Navi Mumbai 400 706
  E-mail: vivamumbai@vivagroupindia.net, Tel. 27721273, 27721274
- Jamals Fazal Chambers, 26 Greams Road, Chennai 600 006
  E-mail: vivachennai@vivagroupindia.net, Tel. 28290304, 28294241
- B-103, Jindal Towers, 21/1A/3 Darga Road, Kolkata 700 017
  E-mail: vivakolkata@vivagroupindia.net, Tel. 22836381, 22816713
- 7, Sovereign Park Apartments, 56-58, K. R. Road, Basavanagudi, Bangalore 560 004
  E-mail: vivabangalore@vivagroupindia.net, Tel. 26607409, 26607410
- 101-102 Mughal Marc Apartments, 3-4-637 to 641, Narayanguda, Hyderabad 500 029
  E-mail: vivahyderabad@vivagroupindia.net, Tel. 27564481, 27564482
- First Floor, Beevi Towers, SRM Road, Kaloor, Kochi 682 018, Kerala
  E-mail: vivakochi@vivagroupindia.net, Tel: 0484-2403055, 2403056

Published by arrangement with

International Self Counsel Press Ltd.
1704 N. State Street
Bellingham WA 98225
USA

ISBN-10: 81-309-0027-0
ISBN-13: 978-81-309-0027-8

Published by Vinod Vasishtha for Viva Books Private Limited, 4737/23, Ansari Road, New Delhi 110 002. Printed and bound by Raj Press, R-3, Inderpuri, New Delhi - 110 012.

To reference librarians everywhere, especially at the Aberdeen Timberland Library, the Prince George Public Library, and the Pierce County Library.

Contents

INTRODUCTION

Market Research Made Easy is written for the first-time, do-it-yourself market researcher. If you are just starting a business or trying to grow your existing small business, this book is for you.

This book will also be helpful if you are in charge of marketing for an established business that still has little budget for research.

In the following chapters, we guide you step by step through your own market research project using a series of worksheets and explanations in nontechnical language. If you begin this book with "real-world" research questions in mind, you can finish the book with real solutions in hand.

There will be times during your project when you might benefit by getting advice from a market research professional. We point out those occasions as we go along. If you decide you want to consult a professional at those points, you'll spend a few hundred dollars, rather than the thousands you'd pay for full-scale professional research. If you choose not to, you can still successfully complete your research entirely on your own.

The best way to demonstrate the effect of market research is to show how a business can actually conduct and use research. Throughout this book, we follow the progress of one young business as it gathers data, analyzes it, and creates its strategy. This particular business is imaginary, but the problems it faces, and the solutions it finds, are drawn from reality.

Market research can be intimidating. But it can also be an exciting trek through worlds of new knowledge — knowledge that can make the difference between success and failure for your business. So relax, enjoy, and prepare to make valuable discoveries.

Chapter 1

WHY RESEARCH YOUR MARKET?

WHAT IS MARKET RESEARCH?

What is market research? It is like —

(a) sticking your big toe in the ocean before jumping in;

(b) stepping lightly on a frozen pond to see if the ice will hold your weight;

(c) tasting a small piece of okra prior to taking a big bite;

(d) test driving a vehicle before obtaining a new car loan; or

(e) trying on a new pair of shoes before buying.

As an individual, doing this kind of "research" could save you all kinds of trouble, from having your feet pinched when you walk to dying of hypothermia.

> Here's an early example of "market research." In 218 B.C., Hannibal of Carthage attacked Rome by crossing the Alps from Spain. He could have used the Carthaginian navy to ferry his troops and baggage across the Mediterranean, thereby attacking Rome directly and at great risk. But instead, Hannibal tested the market first. He sent agents to communities between Spain and Rome. The agents talked with the inhabitants and learned that Rome was very unpopular and that people were fighting mad. Hannibal recognized an opportunity. Instead of attacking directly, he decided to provoke an insurrection that he and his army would lead.

Now put your business hat on. Market research could involve —

(a) learning whether the local economy is going downhill before opening a new upscale dress shop;

(b) doing a patent search before investing $100,000 to manufacture a new electronic game;

(c) finding out whether shoppers are willing to pay $39.99 for your handmade stuffed bunnies before you stitch together four dozen;

(d) calculating whether you can make a profit if it costs 75¢ each to make and market your greeting cards; or

(e) asking customers whether they'd patronize an espresso bar if you added one to your store.

This kind of research could save your business all kinds of trouble, from spending months sewing bunnies that don't sell to getting sued by an outraged patent-holder.

Market research is a child of the industrial age. Once upon a time, if you wanted shoes, you went directly to a cobbler and the cobbler made a pair just for you. When you needed a barrel, the cooper assembled one for you. The cobbler didn't have to make 3,000 pairs of shoes and worry who would or wouldn't buy them. The cooper didn't fret about whether customers would purchase his warehouse full of bushel barrels, or whether they might suddenly demand thousands of peck barrels instead. He didn't have to, because no warehouse full of barrels existed.

Your situation is different. Even if you offer a custom-made, handcrafted product or a one-on-one service, you are in a different marketing era. Chances are you can't anticipate market demand as easily as that cobbler (who could, just by strolling through the village, see who would soon be asking for a new pair of buskins). Chances are you can't always discuss price one-on-one. Chances are you have more competitors and you market your product or service in a larger geographical area to customers who aren't as well known to you. And with the Internet you may find your customers come from around the world.

Market research will help you know your customers and your market just as well as that cobbler did. And once you know your customers, you'll be in the best position to meet their needs — and your own.

Taking aim at a marketing goal doesn't always guarantee you're going to hit the target, but at least you'll be more likely to hit the marketing bull's-eye than to shoot a hole in your foot or your piggy bank. In short, market research is effort you take before a venture that could save you time and money.

HOW DO YOU DO IT?

Market research is simply a process of asking questions or finding existing information about the market, your competition, and potential customers. You need answers to questions such as —

(a) What kind of person is most likely to buy my product?

(b) Are there enough of those people for me to make money?

(c) How can I reach those potential buyers?

(d) Is someone else already fulfilling my potential customers' needs?

Once you have the answers (the data), you then process and analyze them, converting data into information. From this information, you develop a strategy (or plan) for building your company, marketing your product, or meeting whatever other marketing goal you have.

You will go through 11 steps in your marketing research:

1. Brainstorming your marketing idea
2. Forming your hypothesis
3. Identifying the information you need
4. Researching secondary sources
5. Checking your hypothesis
6. Researching primary sources
7. Analyzing/interpreting data
8. Checking your hypothesis again
9. Making your plan
10. Presenting your plan
11. Implementing your plan

Each of these steps are discussed in further detail in later chapters.

THE MOST DIFFICULT THING ABOUT MARKET RESEARCH

The most difficult thing about market research isn't finding or understanding the data. It's that market research can burst bubbles.

> *I'm a slow walker, but I never walk back.*
>
> ABRAHAM LINCOLN

Market research can destroy ideas. It can tell you customers think $99 is an outrageous price for a set of plastic rain gear. It can tell you the corner of Third and Main is a rotten place to put your frozen-yogurt store. It can tell you women won't buy a tool set just because it comes in a pink box (believe it or not, some marketer recently learned that one the hard way, by having women scornfully reject the product after it was on store shelves).

But if you let it, market research can point you toward successful ventures even while demolishing a cherished idea. To approach research in the right spirit, you must never let knowledge discourage you. The more information you possess, the more opportunities you will be able to recognize, and the better you will be able to evaluate them.

WHEN SHOULD YOU DO MARKET RESEARCH?

Before starting a new business

The most important question for any business is, Will someone buy my product or service? In a way, that question is more important than, Does my product work? If you can't sell what you produce, you won't be in business long, no matter how good your product is.

Before beginning a new business, you need to find out the answers to the following questions:

(a) Is there a need for my product or service?

(b) What kind of person is most likely to buy my product or service?

(c) Are there enough of those people in the market area?

(d) How am I going to find those customers?

(e) Is a competitor already meeting their needs?

(f) If so, can I offer something the competitor can't?

(g) How much are buyers willing to pay?

(h) Will finding those buyers cost more than the profit margin will allow?

(i) Is there a profit margin?

> Kathleen Mahoney wanted to have the finest of everything at her wedding, but finding those high-quality items was difficult. She researched everything. She could find no single source of tasteful accessories for an upscale bride. Mahoney began thinking. A bridal business that featured one-stop shopping might be successful. She found out that there were 2.5 million weddings a year in the United States. She surveyed friends. She checked demographics. She borrowed money and in February of 1990, started a successful business, Wedding Fantastic Inc.
>
> *Inc., May, 1992*

When introducing a new product or service

If you own a growing business, at some point you will probably want to add a new service, extend your product line, or add a department to your store. Market research can help you do it successfully and avoid costly mistakes.

By introducing a new product or service without research, you could —

(a) end up with a warehouse full of products that remain unsold;

(b) face a discouraged staff whose calls are constantly rebuffed by customers;

(c) find yourself facing competing products you were unaware of;

> *The best entrepreneurs are risk avoiders. They identify the risk, and then they take actions to minimize its effects.*
>
> Paul Hawken

(d) drain money from your more successful operations; and

(e) even damage your company's reputation.

By introducing a product or service that doesn't complement your product line, you may weaken your image in the customers' mind, or even drive customers away. Cadillac did this when they introduced the low-cost car model Cimaron in the early eighties; the car didn't attract economy car buyers because it was a Cadillac, and it drove "status" car buyers toward high-end European cars, offended that Cadillac had cheapened its image.

By introducing a perfectly good product in the wrong manner, you may do similar harm. That happened to Coca-Cola when they introduced New Coke and pulled their 100-year-old original Coke off the market. The switch enraged millions of consumers. Coke eventually recovered; a smaller business might not have.

Market research is especially important for an expanding business. A brand-new entrepreneur sometimes feels as if he or she has nothing to lose and might as well operate on guts and instinct alone. But your expanding business has plenty to lose: profits, reputation, and even its existence.

To maintain your existing business

The market changes. The competition changes. Technology changes. Customers change. And your business changes with them, whether or not you want it to. The only question is, do you anticipate the changes, watch the new currents and ride with them, or do you stand still and possibly get swept away?

Let's look at an imaginary couple, George and Bertha, who bought a "mom-and-pop" corner store back in 1960. George and Bertha weren't fond of change, so they kept their store pretty much as it was. For a few years, George and Bertha made a good living.

Then, in the mid-sixties, came that new breed of corner store — the 7-11, the Jiffy Mart, and others of their ilk. George and Bertha lost a big chunk of their customer base to the glossy stores with their extended hours, but they still had neighborhood loyalists and they still stayed the same, though they made a little less.

Then came the seventies, and the neighborhood filled with Southeast Asians, relocated after the Vietnam War. They brought a new cuisine and new grocery needs, but George and Bertha didn't understand "all that foreign food," so they continued to stay the same, though they made a little less.

> Sometimes you just get lucky. Southern Audio Services, Inc. began a market reserarch survey by calling a computer store to poll it about its interest in buying a new type of cable. "Yes," replied the store owner — and placed an order. One call, one order. Southern Audio went straight into production.
>
> *Inc., September, 1992*

Then came the eighties, and the few remaining old neighborhood people began to move to retirement homes. A growing colony of yuppies came in, attracted by the neighborhood's quaint charm. This "gentrification" brought a demand for espresso, exotic pastas, jicama, and kiwi fruit. But George and Bertha didn't know anything about "all that nonsense." So they stayed the same.

Now they made a lot less than they used to. In fact, not enough to keep the store open. In the early nineties, they sold their store for next-to-nothing to a young Vietnamese immigrant who was soon doing a booming business in spices, teas, and coffees.

George and Bertha remained proud of the fact that their store had never changed but, of course, it had changed. It had died.

The best way to keep your existing business "the same" is to keep it consistently profitable, consistently on top of its market. That's where market research comes in. It helps you know what your customers want now and how their wants are changing. It can also help you fine-tune your business, improving service here, upgrading your signage there, putting a new twist on advertising, all in response to what existing (and potential) customers want.

> *It is characteristic of wisdom not to do desperate things.*
>
> Henry David Thoreau

You may think you already know your customers and potential customers. Maybe so. But time and again we've found that the business person — like the cheated-upon spouse — is often the last to know. You might be like a restaurant owner we knew who was very proud of his food and had no idea that his customers were just as much in love with his convenient parking. When he closed a section of the parking lot to expand the restaurant, his customers went elsewhere. He should have asked what they really valued.

If you own an existing business, you need to know

(a) how customers and potential customers perceive your product or service;

(b) how that perception has changed over time;

(c) if there is a new, untapped market for your existing products or services;

(d) if your existing customer base is ready for a new product or service you could provide;

(e) if your prices are in line with current needs;

(f) if there is new technology which could enhance or destroy your business;

(g) if the members of your target market are aging, growing younger, getting richer or poorer; and

(h) if competitors are meeting needs you are not.

Case Study

Clarice Rogers is a business person in her early thirties. While her children were young, she took up calligraphy as a hobby. Now she sells one-of-a-kind cards, wall hangings, and other objects at craft fairs. The fairs, however, involve weekend work and travel and, for some time, Clarice has been looking for an opportunity to manage her calligraphy business in a more professional, entrepreneurial manner.

To her surprise, the opportunity may have arisen in the form of an elegant, hand-bound appointment calendar she made as a present to herself. Everyone who has seen the little book has clamored over its beauty and usefulness. Finally, one friend suggested, "You could sell one of those to every woman executive in the country!" And that set Clarice to thinking.

She took the book to several printers and binderies to learn what it would cost to reproduce it by the thousands. Though the price made her gasp, she realized that if she could market the book well, she could make many times that amount, possibly go on to create an entire line of luxury office supplies, and earn her freedom from the craft fair circuit.

But is there a market for her product?

Chapter 2
LAYING THE GROUNDWORK

> *The study and knowledge of the universe would somehow be lame and defective were no practical results to follow.*
>
> CICERO

THE FOUR BASIC PURPOSES OF MARKET RESEARCH

When you start thinking about your own market research project, it can be pretty daunting. There are so many things you need to know, so many questions to ask. It might help to know that, according to *American Demographics* magazine <www.americandemographics.com>, there are just four basic purposes of market research. They are the following:

(a) Analyzing the market

(b) Analyzing the market's response to your product or service

(c) Analyzing the effectiveness of your advertising or promotion

(d) Strategic planning

As you read through the descriptions below, note down those questions you most need the answers to.

Analyzing the market

Market analysis research helps you assess the market potential of a new product, service, or business. It can also help you choose sites for a new business or outlet. Market analysis can answer questions such as the following:

- What groups of people are present in the market?
- Are there enough members of my target group to make the business worthwhile?

- How large is the potential market?
- Realistically, how much of that potential can I capture?
- Who are my likely customers?
- Where will my customers come from?
- Who are the competition's customers?
- How can I attract more customers?
- What is the best location for my business?

Analyzing the market's response to your product or service

This kind of analysis is intended to calculate your product's or service's potential in the market. These studies can (and probably should) be conducted before a product is introduced. But you can also conduct this type of survey later to improve your marketing or your product.

Product or service studies answer questions such as the following:

- Who are the best customers for my product or service?
- How much and how often do they buy?
- What will they pay for my product, and at that rate, can I make a profit?
- What are their needs for the product or service?
- How does my product or service meet their needs?
- How are my customers changing?
- How are their needs for my product or service changing?
- Can I alter the product or service to better meet their needs?

While this type of research sounds similar in some ways to a market analysis study, the market study looks at the overall characteristics of the market, while a product or service analysis examines how the market is likely to respond to your specific product or service.

By asking the right questions, you can find out not only *how* customers or potential customers respond to your offerings, but *who* is responding *in what way* and *how much money* different types of buyers are spending. For instance, you could learn that women aged 25 to 34 are spending twice as much money on your product as women in any other age group; that would help you target your market to them in the future. Or you may learn that men 18 to 34 are not using your service because they don't understand it well enough; if that group is important to you, you could use the information to simplify the service or simplify your explanation of the service.

> *To treat your facts with imagination is one thing, but to imagine your facts is another.*
>
> John Burroughs

Analyzing the effectiveness of your advertising or promotion

This research helps you develop a message that will get your customers' attention and sell them your goods or services. Such studies can also help you select the most effective and most cost-effective advertising medium.

Here's what you can find out with an advertising or promotional study:

- What advertising or promotional message will get the best results from my customers?
- What methods or messages will most powerfully induce people to buy?
- Does my advertising or promotion help create the image I want customers to have when they think of my product or service?
- What advertising medium can best reach my customers?
- Will a combination of media optimize my sales?

Strategic planning

Strategic planning studies track the growth or decline of existing markets and help you discover what products or services (new or existing) will be successful in those markets. Strategic planning research is most likely to be conducted by established firms.

The following questions can be answered by this type of study:

- How are my customers changing?
- How are all segments of the market changing?
- What are the fastest-growing markets or customer groups?
- Are there new products or services they will want that I can deliver?
- What sales growth can I expect from my existing market?
- In which departments or new lines of business should I increase my investment?

As you can see by the questions, there is some overlap between the types of studies; at least three of the studies deal with identifying customers or potential customers.

YOUR TWO SOURCES OF DATA

All market research data comes from one of two sources:

(a) Primary sources

(b) Secondary sources

Don't be misled. In this case, primary does not mean *first* or *more important* and secondary does not mean *second* or *less important.*

Primary data

Primary data is data you generate for your own business. It can come from your customers, potential customers, employees, suppliers, consultants, and other sources involved in your business. You get primary data when you have customers fill out a survey card, when you hold a group discussion (a focus group), or when you talk to customers about your package designs or advertising.

Primary data usually costs money to generate; anywhere from a few dollars for some postcard-sized forms and postage to hundreds of thousands for sophisticated surveys conducted by professionals.

Secondary data

Secondary data is already there for the taking or buying. This includes government census reports, economic and production data, information from news organizations, surveys by trade associations, etc. It comes from sources outside your business and while it does not contain specific information about your business, it may contain valuable information about your potential customers, competitors, suppliers, and many other things that affect your business.

One business's primary data can become another's secondary data. Once data is generated and published by one company (primary), it can be used by others (secondary).

Here are some examples of secondary versus primary data:

Secondary data	**Primary data**
(From a census report): 4,200 women ages 18 to 34 live in Adams City.	(From a market response survey conducted for a mall): The number one reason women shop at the Adams Mall is convenience.

One of the first things Michael Harris did after he took over the presidency of Deck House was to conduct a customer survey. The responses showed buyers were happy with their custom-designed houses, but not with the design and construction process. Deck House had been promoting itself with the slogan, "The choice is yours!" But buyers perceived there were too many choices. After reviewing the surveys, Deck House designed a new line of standardized homes and in one year went from 75 percent custom-designed homes to 75 percent standardized. The company is now able to build more homes with lower overhead (and lower prices!). President Harris is planning a new survey to make sure the customer's wishes lead the company.

INC., NOVEMBER, 1992

(From a government trade report): Profits in the metal fabricating industry rose by 7 percent per year during the 1980s.

(From an advertising analysis study conducted for a metal fabricator): When asked which metal fabricating firm they preferred to buy from, engineers named ConCor two to one over Stone Steelworks.

> *Do not put your faith in what statistics say until you have carefully considered what they do not say.*
>
> WILLIAM W. WATT

In your research, you may use both types of data. Of the four purposes for research mentioned above — market analysis, product or service analysis, advertising or promotion analysis, and strategic planning — the first probably relies most heavily on secondary research; much of what you need to know about the population, its income, its interests, and its buying patterns is already available through published information.

On the other hand, analyzing the effectiveness of your advertising will almost certainly require using primary data; after all, it's *your* advertising you need to analyze.

THE TWO KINDS OF DATA

There are two general types of data:

(a) Quantitative

(b) Qualitative

Quantitative data

Quantitative data is data that can be expressed as quantities, percentages, or numbers. Take another look at the examples of primary and secondary data above. This is the kind of data you get from questionnaires that ask multiple choice questions or require people to rank your service on a scale. It's also the kind of data you get from economic or census reports.

Qualitative data

The statement "The number one reason women shop at the Adams Mall is convenience" is an example of qualitative data, "fuzzy" data about people's feelings and perceptions. There is no way to turn this statement into numbers.

The following customer comments are also examples of qualitative data:

(a) I felt welcome from the moment I arrived at your check-in desk.

(b) The design just isn't as sophisticated as it should be.

(c) Your service stinks.

(d) I think your store is only for little old ladies.

This is the kind of data you get from focus groups (group discussions with members of your target audience) or when you use a questionnaire that allows people space to write comments in their own words. It's also the kind of data you get in day-to-day contact with people in your business.

Just as primary and secondary data both have a place in your research, so do quantitative and qualitative data. Quantitative data is wonderful for helping you understand the big picture of who your customers are and what they're doing. It can be easily compiled into lists and graphs. Qualitative data, on the other hand, can't be charted and isn't statistically meaningful, but is great for giving you insights into the psychological subtleties of your customers' motivations.

UNDERSTANDING DEMOGRAPHICS AND PSYCHOGRAPHICS

When studying groups of people — and that's what 90 percent of market research is — you need to understand what the terms *demographics* and *psychographics* mean.

Demographics

Demographics are relatively simple. They encompass the statistical characteristics of populations. Age, race, gender, religion, income, number of years of schooling, and type of job are all demographic characteristics. So is data describing club memberships, credit cards held, type of car owned, size of house, and size of household. Demographic characteristics are "Just the facts, Ma'am," items that can be measured in numbers or put into simple, obvious categories.

> For a fascinating look at how psychographics are used by the "Big Guys" in the world of advertising, read *The Image Makers* by William Meyers (New York Times Books, 1984). Meyers shows how advertisers group us according to our values and lifestyles, then aim their ads straight past our rational, critical minds and into our hearts. Once you know the psychographics of your own audience, you can use the same techniques to gain the emotinal support of your target audience.

Psychographics

Psychographics are more subtle and describe what groups of people *care about*, how they *feel*, what they *value* and how they *live*. Table 1 shows the difference between these two types of information.

Psychographic information derives from demographic information. Once you have identified the demographic groups that interest you, you can then turn your attention to their psychographic characteristics.

The most effective marketing strategies use psychographics to reach the target audience. After all, if you want to sell BMWs (or teddy bears or computers) you need to know why and how people decide to buy them. There are a lot of books and studies that explain the psychographics of various groups, but the best way to learn the psychographics of your target audience is by talking to them, observing them, and applying your own common sense to what you see.

GETTING TO KNOW YOUR TARGET CUSTOMER

> *It's not who you know, it's what you know about them.*
>
> AMERICAN DEMOGRAPHICS

Who's your best potential customer — your target? A lot of your research involves finding out where your target lives, how he or she buys, what he or she earns, thinks, and does. You can't learn any of this until you know exactly who the target is.

Who's my target? may seem like an obvious question, but in fact, it can be one of the most difficult questions a small business person has to answer. Many business owners will give an answer like this:

- Men
- Women
- Men and women
- Business people
- Adults

But your best target customer is someone much more specific than that. Since 80 percent of your business will probably come from 20 percent of your customers, one of your first priorities is to figure out (or find out) everything you should know about that 20 percent — your true target market. For example, if both men and women purchase from you, but men outnumber women three to one, then your target is almost certainly male. If both college students and high school students would love your product, but college students buy twice as much, then college students are probably your target.

Using nothing but your existing knowledge, fill out Worksheet 1 to generate some data about your target customer. Your later research will help you confirm or refine the thinking you do here. Following the worksheet is Sample 1, which shows how Clarice, of our case study, described her target customer.

In answering the last question, keep in mind the distinction between a *benefit* and a *feature*. Identify the emotional or psychological fulfillment you give customers (the benefit), not the specific product or service you sell them (the feature).

After finishing this exercise, you should have a mental image of your customer as specific as: My target is an executive woman homeowner in her forties, or, My target is a male college student with an eye for high-tech electronic gear. Although you have created this first picture using "gut instinct," it can be verified or modified later by the information you generate as a result of your research.

By identifying your customers this specifically, you are not excluding anyone. A wide range of people can still buy from you. But the better you identify your customers, the better you will be able to gear your products and services to their needs. The better you know your customers, the easier it will be to find them and appeal to them.

TABLE 1
COMPARISON OF PSYCHOGRAPHIC AND DEMOGRAPHIC INFORMATION

POTENTIAL CUSTOMERS	DEMOGRAPHIC INFORMATION	PSYCHOGRAPHIC INFORMATION
of a BMW Dealership	Married 30 to 40 year olds $50,000 to $100,000 family income Own their own homes	Status seekers Professionals Upwardly mobile
of a SAAB Dealership	Married 30 to 50 year olds $50,000 to $100,000 family income Own their own homes	Socially conscious Politically liberal
of a GEO Dealership	Unmarried 20 to 30 year olds $20,000 to $30,000 income Rent home or apartment	Practical Budget-minded

Case Study

To find out whether there is a market for her appointment book, Clarice Rogers determines to do some market research. It's clear to her that this research will serve two fundamental purposes:

(a) Analyzing the market

(b) Analyzing the market's response to her product

She needs to study the market because she isn't really sure who her target audience is and where buyers might come from. Is her market truly executive women? And if so, are there enough such women locally? Or will Clarice need to market to a wider geographic area?

She needs to analyze the market's response to her product because she is considering investing tens of thousands of dollars in printing, binding, and advertising costs. She needs to know whether the design of the book is acceptable to buyers, what price point to select, how many books she might be able to sell, and why and how people might choose to purchase.

She begins by drawing a mental picture of the person she believes is her target, and concludes the target customer exercise as shown in Sample 1.

WORKSHEET 1
DESCRIBING YOUR TARGET CUSTOMER

Gender (male/female):	
Age range (child, teen, young adult, middle age, senior):	
Occupation type (white-collar, blue-collar, sales, service, student, business owner, retired):	
Specific occupation (if important):	
Home owner (if important):	
Income range:	
Hobbies and interests:	
Other important characteristics:	
Main benefit this customer gets from choosing your product or service:	

SAMPLE 1
DESCRIBING YOUR TARGET CUSTOMER

Gender (male/female):	Female
Age range (child, teen, young adult, middle age, senior):	25 to 49
Occupation type (white-collar, blue-collar, sales, service, student, business owner, retired):	White-collar business executive or owner
Specific occupation (if important):	Any type of desk/office-oriented job
Home owner (if important):	Yes
Income range:	$40,000+
Hobbies and interests:	Art? Interior Decorating?
Other important characteristics:	Very interested in quality and aesthetics
Main benefit this customer gets from choosing your product or service:	This woman feels more organized and more pampered when she uses this book

THE ELEMENTS OF MARKET RESEARCH

Three times when you need market research

- Before starting a new business
- When introducing a new product or service
- To maintain your existing business

+

Four basic purposes of market research

- Analyzing the market
- Analyzing the market's response to your product
- Analyzing your advertising effectiveness
- Strategic planning

+

Two sources of data

- Primary
- Secondary

+

Two kinds of data

- Quantitative
- Qualitative

=

The success of your business

Chapter 3
SETTING YOUR RESEARCH DIRECTION

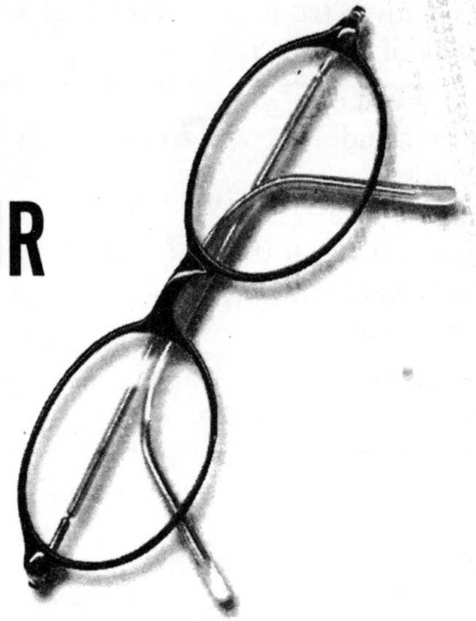

> *When markets shift, technologies proliferate, competitors multiply, and products become obsolete almost overnight, successful companies are those that consistently create new knowledge, disseminate it widely throughout the organization, and quickly embody it in new technologies and products.*
>
> IKUJIRO NONAKA

CLEAR THE AIR WITH A BRAINSTORM

The first step in research is to ask yourself, What are the questions I need answers to?

You could come up with a list of questions by sitting down with a pencil and paper, tapping ideas into your computer, or checking items from the lists given in chapter 2. But by doing that, you may be unintentionally neglecting some very interesting and productive areas of research.

One of the best ways to produce a variety of ideas and, ultimately, the right marketing research questions, is to get ideas from a variety of other people through a brainstorming session.

Brainstorming means getting a group of creative, articulate people together in a room and letting ideas rip. It is *the* best way to make sure you have a lot of different ideas for developing your product, service, or company, or to set the direction of your research.

Choosing your participants

If you are going into business for the first time, your brainstorming crew may be family members, friends, partners, potential customers, potential suppliers, and possibly a volunteer from a business self-help organization like the Service Corps of Retired

Executives (SCORE) (United States) or the Business Development Bank of Canada (BDC) (Canada).

If you own or manage an existing business, your brainstormers may include employees, managers, customers, suppliers, ad agency representatives, or freelance creative people. You may even want to throw in a ringer, someone who has nothing to do with your business, but who you know to be a creative thinker. You do not necessarily want your brainstorming group made up of members of your target audience; the more mixed the group, the better.

In most cases, you do not need to pay people to participate, but judge by your own circumstances and by how much you are asking of your brainstorm team.

Here are some qualities to look for in members of your brainstorming team:

(a) *Broad-minded.* Don't choose people who are rigid or easily offended.

(b) *Independent.* You want people who will give you their ideas without regard to personal relationships. Also, look for people who don't have a vested interest in a particular plan or path.

(c) *Fun-loving.* Your people should bat ideas around like a puppy playing with a ball.

(d) *Original.* They should give you unusual slants and observations.

(e) *Prolific.* Don't choose someone who hardly ever speaks. The more ideas you hear the better.

(f) *Outgoing.* Use people who aren't afraid of getting up and playing a role or even singing, if the mood is right.

> *The value of an idea has nothing whatsoever to do with the sincerity of the man who expresses it.*
>
> OSCAR WILDE

Choosing the facilitator

The facilitator is critical to the success of the session. Pick an enthusiastic, unintimidating person to play this role. If yours is an established company, the facilitator should probably not be a CEO or a department head, who might overwhelm employees or suppliers who are present. A member of the sales staff might be a good facilitator, or someone who works in marketing or communications.

You might also consider going outside the company to find a facilitator. Business schools and colleges may have staff or faculty appropriate for the task. Or consider hiring a consultant from a marketing or public relations firm.

If you are just getting started and/or have no money to hire a facilitator, a SCORE or BDC adviser could help, or you could do it yourself if you have the right personality.

Before settling on the facilitator, especially if you are bringing in a volunteer or consultant from outside the company, talk with the person to be sure that you will get what you need from the sessions. If you are hiring a consultant, ask to see a marketing plan or finished report the consultant has put together. Will the consultant only lead the discussion or will you be expecting a written report and suggestions for future paths? You should decide this in advance.

> Many years ago 3M Corporation developed a "useless" glue. Objects glued with it could be picked up and stuck down over and over again without the glue losing its tackiness. But as a glue, it just wasn't sticky enough, thought the product designers. So the product was put on the shelf. It was not until a 3M employee, tired of having bookmarks slip out of his hymnal at church choir practice, applied some of the glue to little bits of paper, that anyone realized they had a useful product. Applied to paper and sold as Post-It Notes, it became the biggest selling product the company has ever produced — outselling event the famous Scotch Magic Tape. The glue developers had been too married to their preconceived ideas about glue to realize what they'd created. It took one person with a "crazy" idea about how to use the product to bring out the product's true potential.

Running the brainstorming session

While there are many schools of thought on how to conduct a brainstorming session, the basics are incredibly simple:

(a) Gather people who can present ideas in a positive way; avoid nay-sayers.

(b) Appoint a moderator or facilitator who can subtly guide the discussion.

(c) Appoint someone to take notes during the session and prepare a report afterward.

(d) Have a general idea of what you want to accomplish but no preconceived notions about what conclusions you'll reach.

(e) Set up a chalkboard, marker board, or large pad of paper for the moderator to write on; have several colored markers or chalks handy.

(f) Keep the discussion wide open; encourage people to speak up; don't impose turn-taking, hand-raising or any other form of order (but if one or two people dominate the conversation, do have the moderator make sure others have a chance to be heard).

(g) Allow enough time for chemistry to develop and ideas to flow; two hours is a good length. If you have a lot to discuss, try several two-hour sessions with breaks between them. An hour is probably not long enough.

(h) And remember, THERE IS NO SUCH THING AS A BAD IDEA.

The early part of a brainstorming session is usually dedicated to throwing out a wide and wild range of ideas on a given subject (e.g., How could a person use this widget?). At some point, when the page is full, when participants have run dry, or when a preestablished amount of time has elapsed, the moderator will narrow the discussion, perhaps by letting the brainstormers pick several of the most promising ideas and develop them further.

We can't overemphasize this: Don't hold back anything. Never pooh-pooh an idea, even if it seems preposterous. A snide comment, a bad pun, or an off-the-wall concept could lead to someone else's brilliant observation. Encourage everyone and write everything down. You are prospecting. And you may not know until later which nuggets are "real" gold.

A good way to get ideas from everyone, even people who are shy, is to have people write their ideas down on 3" x 5" cards. The cards are given to a facilitator. No one knows who suggested what. This is an excellent way to initiate comments and handle employee inhibitions.

When holding a brainstorming session to start your marketing research, you may want to begin by asking questions as basic as these:

(a) What is the product? (Let the brainstormers tell you. You may be surprised.)

(b) How could the product be used?

(c) Who would use it?

(d) Why would these people use this product for this purpose?

Look for alternatives:

(a) What can be done about our ... ?

(b) What would happen if ... ?

(c) Could this be simplified by ... ?

(d) How practical is it to ... ?

(e) What could possibly go wrong?

A dictionary is a fun tool to use in brainstorming. If you have a problem to solve and your team runs out of ideas, pick up the dictionary, open it to any page, and choose any word at random. Ask people to come up with solutions that the word brings to mind. For example, How can we simplify this product, "perpendicularly"?

One day Alice came to a fork in the road and saw a Cheshire Cat in a tree. "Which road do I take?" she asked. His response was a question: "Where do you want to go?" "I don't know," Alice answered. "Then," said the cat, "it doesn't matter."

LEWIS CARROLL

Two things a brainstorming session can do for you

Let's say you go into your brainstorming session with questions like these:

(a) We think we have a great product here ... but who is most likely to use it?

(b) We've developed an attache case with a built-in voice to remind execs of their appointments; what should we call it?

(c) Do you think the market is ready for day-glo underwear?

(d) What other kinds of businesses might sign up for an 800-number referral service like doctors and dentists sometimes use?

There are at least two ways your brainstorming session can help you with such questions:

(a) Give you further directions for research

(b) Give you answers to questions

A Gateway Computer print ad featuring buffalo came out about the same time as the movie *Dances with Wolves*. The ad brought a large response to the mail-order firm. At their next brainstorming session, someone joked that they should check into Kevin Costner's next movie project. The next movie was *Robin Hood*. The Gateway Computer ad featuring Robin Hood set company records for orders.

Inc., July, 1992

Give you further directions for research

If you asked the question above about who might use a new 800-number referral service, your brainstormers might suggest auto repair shops, maid services, computer repair businesses, and escort services. Rather than going out and marketing to these diverse businesses, you would first conduct research to find out how many of those businesses there are in your potential market area, what interest they would have in a referral service, how much they would be willing to pay, how much it would cost you to set up the service, and (in the case of the escort services!) whether you might be breaking any laws or flaunting any codes of ethics by establishing your business.

Give you answers to questions

The brainstorming session can sometimes directly give you the answers you need. If you were looking for a name for that talking attaché case, for instance, and your brainstorming team suggested Justin Case, The Walkie-Talkie, Attaché Today, The Voice that Toured, and The Space Case, you might find the name you like right in that bunch. (You would still be wise to search the databases to discover whether anyone else owns your chosen name, and to test several names with members of your target market.)

You may come out of the session with some very specific areas to work on in your research, or you may end up with just pages and pages of new ideas to play with. But in any case, you'll certainly come away with more than you could have if you'd put even an exceptionally insightful person alone in a room with paper and pencil.

> *Skill is fine, and genius is splendid, but the right contacts are more valuable than either.*
>
> SIR ARCHIBALD MCINDOE

FORMING YOUR HYPOTHESIS

Using the ideas you generated through the brainstorming session, you can now begin to form a hypothesis. A hypothesis is a working assumption, a proposition that you will test during the course of your research. It gives you a specific direction to go and specific things to look for. You begin with a proposition, then collect evidence that proves, disproves, or modifies it.

Here are some examples of market research hypotheses:

(a) Our talking briefcase will be used primarily by young executives attracted to electronic gadgetry; while most of these potential users will be male, many of the purchasers will be upscale wives and girlfriends, buying the cases as gifts.

(b) Auto repair shops will subscribe to my proposed 1-800 referral service if they perceive the price to be affordable and if paperwork can be kept to a minimum.

(c) Teenagers will purchase day-glo underwear from my company if it is positioned as being a radical, rebellious, sexy thing to do.

Each of these hypotheses gives the marketer of the product in question a specific research goal to work on. It is possible research will prove the hypothesis wrong. It is more likely research will lead to the refinement of the hypothesis. For example, auto repair shops will subscribe to a 1-800 referral service if the price is less than $30 per month or 5 percent of any referral.

> In 1911, a young meteorologist named Alfred Wegener conceived the idea that the earth's continents had all once been part of a single land mass and had since drifted apart. This flew in the face of all conventional geological thinking, which said that continents and seas were fixed and unchanging. But Wegener used his idea as a hypothesis, then began examining the physical evidence: identical fossils found thousands of miles apart, the odd "fit" in the Atlantic coastlines of South America and Africa, and dozens of other factors. After Wegener and many other scientists had examined the evidence, his hypothesis was accepted.

IDENTIFYING THE INFORMATION YOU NEED

With your hypothesis in hand, you can now come up with a coherent list of specific things you need to learn. Use Worksheet 2 to record your questions. For example, working with hypothesis (a) from the list above, you might make a list like this:

(a) What age group is most likely to use the talking briefcase?

(b) Is it accurate to assume most users will be men?

(c) What age group is most likely to purchase the briefcase?

(d) What are the demographics of typical briefcase purchasers?

(e) Are there certain types of business people to whom this briefcase might have particular appeal (e.g., computer company executives)?

(f) What will they be willing to pay?

(g) Will the case sell better if it is made of leather, vinyl, or some form of high-tech metal or plastic?

(h) What product name will have the most appeal to the target audience?

(i) What advertising vehicles will best reach our target audience?

(j) What competing products exist?

(k) How should we position this case against the competition?

Your list may be longer or shorter. Once you have completed it, you are ready to begin digging for the data you need to answer your questions. The basic research questions resulting from Clarice's brainstorming group are shown in Sample 2.

WORSHEET 2
FORMULATING YOUR BASIC RESEARCH QUESTIONS

Hypothesis and Basic Questions

My business/product/service is: ____________________

The hypothesis I want to test is: ____________________

____

____

#	Basic Research Questions	Answers (to be filled in later)
1.		
2.		
3.		
4.		
5.		
6.		
7.		
8.		
9.		
10.		
11.		
12.		

Case Study

Clarice assembles a brainstorming group of two artist friends, a sales rep from a printing company, two members of a local business women's organization, and, for a few off-the-wall ideas, her 11-year-old son. This group, she decides, is diverse enough to assure a wide range of thoughts, yet has enough knowledge to produce ideas well-grounded in reality. A volunteer from a business self-help group moderates the session.

The session starts slowly. As group members pass the book around the table, Clarice senses that some doubt its market potential. She has already shared her own fears with the moderator in private: Is it too expensive? Too impractical? But the moderator kicks off the session with a question that bypasses those doubts and gets the creative juices flowing: "If you were this book, where would I find you?"

"Department stores," someone volunteers. "On a big mahogany desk." "An art supply store." "A fancy boudoir." "In my briefcase," counters one of the businesswomen.

The oddball question serves its purpose. Pretty soon the group has transcended any doubts and entered the realm of creative marketing. They decide the book would most likely be found on the big mahogany desk, then they go on to draw a mental picture of the person sitting at the desk: a 40-something woman executive, who wears suits from upscale stores, cooks gourmet dinners for friends, and drives an Acura or an Infiniti.

Everyone knows the actual user of the book could be very different, but creating a strong image of an ideal user of the book helps them discuss some vital questions: Would she buy it herself or would she receive it as a gift? Would she buy it for others? Where might she shop for it? What kind of package would attract her? What price? Why would she choose it?

The group is unanimous in believing that the book's target market is upscale executive women. They believe the product has equally strong potential to be bought as a gift by the end user. But they can't agree on where or how women would be most likely to purchase it. After some discussion, they narrow it down to three possibilities: ads in working women's magazines, direct mail, or upscale department stores.

Clarice leaves the session with a variety of new ideas and a sense that many of her own gut feelings have been validated. After the session she sorts through the huge sheets of paper on which the moderator wrote everyone's ideas. From the most commonly agreed-upon ideas she writes her hypothesis and list of basic questions to research.

SAMPLE 2
FORMULATING YOUR BASIC RESEARCH QUESTIONS

Hypothesis and Basic Questions

My business/product/service is: *Calligraphy Book of Days*

The hypothesis I want to test is: *This product will be used by executives and other upscale executive women and will be purchased by them for their own use and for gifts.*

#	Basic Research Questions	Answers (to be filled in later)
1.	*Is this truly my market?*	
2.	*Are there enough members of my target locally?*	
3.	*How much will people pay?*	
4.	*Can I make enough profit to earn a living?*	
5.	*What is the chief benefit people get from this product?*	
6.	*Are there any competing products on the market?*	
7.	*If so, what can I offer that they don't?*	
8.	*How can I reach my target market?*	
9.	*Could I — or would I want to — sell the book through upscale department stores?*	
10.		
11.		
12.		

Chapter 4

SECONDARY DATA: WHAT'S AVAILABLE?

> *Knowledge is of two kinds. We know a subject ourselves, or we know where we can find information upon it.*
>
> SAMUEL JOHNSON

WHAT KIND OF DATA CAN YOU EXPECT TO FIND?

This chapter and the next will help you gather data from secondary sources. You may find that secondary data will provide all the answers you need to launch your new business, product, or service. In most cases, though, secondary data will save you money, help you refine your hypothesis, and help you narrow your list of questions when it's time to conduct primary research.

Here are some of the types of data you can expect to get from secondary sources:

(a) Demographic statistics
(b) Scientific study data
(c) Media survey data
(d) Public polls
(e) Patent and trademark data
(f) Legal information
(g) Addresses and phone numbers
(h) Information on business procedures
(i) Prices and specifications

Some of what we list in this chapter may not fall neatly under the headings of quantitative and qualitative data, for instance, addresses, legal information, and product specifications. But it's all information you can use in your market research and marketing efforts.

Demographic statistics

Demographic statistics are everywhere. Examples include the number of women over age 65 living in Newfoundland, the total value of the California date crop in 2002, average household income in Manhattan, and the number of people in Vancouver owning licensed dogs.

Such statistics are commonly published by government agencies, but may also come from chambers of commerce, economic development bureaus, universities, and other sources. While none of the above examples may be even remotely useful to you, similar statistics are available from published sources about your market.

Scientific study data

From scientific study data published in various journals, by trade associations, or by large corporations, you can glean such potentially valuable marketing data as how consumption of aspirin affects men who have had heart attacks, how early detection improves the cure rate of breast cancer, what health regimens work best to prevent the long-term devastation of diabetes, and whether certain foods or types of exercise appear to prolong life.

In other words, these are valuable sources of information for marketers of food, athletic gear, diet programs, drugs, vitamins, etc.

Media survey data

Media surveys come in both national and local varieties and cover such territory as the number of men aged 18 to 49 who watch *The Tonight Show* in a given week, the average minutes per day women spend reading the newspaper, the average readership of one trade magazine versus its competitors, and whether a print ad with color has greater reader recall than one in black and white.

These surveys are conducted by the individual media or by professional survey organizations such as Neilsen and ARBitron (United States) and the Bureau of Broadcast Measurement (BBM) (Canada).

Public polls

Polls are conducted by magazines, newspapers, TV networks, research groups, online search engines, and sometimes by colleges

> Two ads in a recent magazine tell an interesting demographic story. One offers a free trial subscription to *The Boomer Report*, "the newsletter that monitors the baby boom generation, what they're buying, thinking, feeling, and doing next." Below, a research/direct marketing firm offers its knowledge of adults over 50, the market that, the ad says, "earns more than half the country's disposable income." There is something for everyone. You can probably find a data research firm that processes information on your prime target customers.
>
> *American Demographics*, August, 1992

and universities. These polls can tell you things such as whether people in Oregon are becoming more politically conservative, what percentage of 18-year-olds are sexually active, whether shoppers in Calgary plan to spend more or less this Christmas season, or whether business owners in Ohio plan to spend more or less on capital projects in the coming year.

Patent and trademark data

Patent and trademark data can tell you what competitors are doing or plan to be doing in the near future. It can inspire your own ideas by showing you what others have done. But most important, it can help assure that your planned product, logo, or name isn't already someone else's property. It is extremely important to do a patent search before investing money and time to manufacture a new product. You could end up getting sued if you don't. It is equally important to conduct a trademark search before rolling out a new brand name, product name, company name, etc., particularly if you will be marketing nationally or over a large geographic region. This information is maintained by the federal government; thousands of the best-known trademarks are also published in many privately published directories and art books.

Legal information

You can expect to find information about laws and regulations that affect your product, service, or business. This information is published by governmental agencies at all levels.

Addresses and phone numbers

Addresses and phone numbers are available by the thousands or tens of thousands from many sources. You can obtain addresses or phone numbers for government offices, trade associations, media, manufacturers, competitors, you name it. Follow these up and they'll lead you to even more data.

Information on business procedures

Want to export to Taiwan? Import from Ireland? You can easily find publications that outline the procedures. Interested in franchising? There are manuals and directories to tell you how to do it, and how to locate franchise operations.

Prices and specifications

There are a number of directories that offer prices and specifications on manufactured products, media, and services. While you should never use these prices without personally verifying them, they can serve as a general guide to help your planning.

LIES, DAMNED LIES, AND STATISTICS

All types of data can be valuable. For example, let's say you own a sporting goods store and are planning to open a branch in another area. You think Prince George, BC, looks like a good market, but you don't know the city or its people very well. Data from Statistics Canada can give you basic information about population, gender, age and other demographic characteristics. The *Gale Directory of Publications & Broadcast Media* can help you locate information about local media and rates; the media themselves can supply you with more information about market characteristics and media audiences. The local chamber of commerce or regional development board can supply you with information about retailers already in the market. All this for the price of a few phone calls or a few minutes at the library.

Statistics are no substitute for judgment.

HENRY CLAY

But all data must be viewed with some caution. This is particularly true of polls that rely on unsupported statements by interviewees and studies produced by people who have a vested interest in the outcome.

Let's say you are marketing products or services to teens, and you find a survey which announces that 87 percent of all 18-year-olds are sexually active. This may alarm you if you are promoting Christian youth groups; it may delight you if you manufacture condoms imprinted with pictures of rock stars. But in either case, you must ask yourself how reliable this information really is. Was it obtained by simply asking kids about their sex lives? If so, how many 18-year-olds do you think would really tell the truth ... and how many might lie to seem more cool? How defined were the questions and the terms of the survey?

People should think things out fresh and not just accept conventional terms and the conventional way of doing things.

BUCKMINSTER FULLER

Media surveys are among the most unreliable. Nationally, different survey methods have produced widely differing ratings, calling the accuracy of all surveys into question. Local surveys, taken during selected "sweeps weeks," are often thrown off balance when one station or publication conducts a red-hot but entirely temporary promotional campaign, usually a contest with a huge prize. In addition, local media can be absolutely shameless in their *interpretation* of the surveys, selectively pulling out data to prove that "We're number one!"

You should be aware of the sponsorship of "scientific" studies. Industry groups such as tobacco, dairy, wood products, pharmaceutical, cosmetic, and many others often sponsor studies, some of which are valid and some of which are merely self-serving.

Even scientific studies can be flawed; like the much-ballyhooed study a few years ago that claimed oat bran reduced cholesterol. The men in the study eating oat bran did indeed have lower cholesterol. But it turned out to be because they weren't eating bacon, sausage, and eggs, not because they were eating oat bran.

Sometimes the accuracy of your data is critical. Other times, the *perception* is all that matters. If consumers say they will be buying more high-ticket items this Christmas, and you crank up production of your $750 hand-carved rocking horses, you can go down in flames if consumers decide to make this a Kmart year. On the other hand, marketers of oat products did very well for a while on the *public perception* of oat bran's miraculous powers, even though the study that "proved" oat bran's powers was flawed.

GETTING THE REAL GOODS

To confront a person with his shadow is to show him his own light.

CARL YUNG

If the data is unreliable, is your research project of any use? Few of us are in a position to judge the validity of a scientific study methodology or the makeup of a survey group. Here are three things that will help assure the accuracy of your data:

(a) Get as much data as you can

(b) Apply your own common sense to it

(c) Decide whether you have enough to make a decision

Get as much data as you can

Find out everything you can about demographics, psychographics, buying patterns, economic conditions, possible trends — whatever data you need. When a particular bit of data is crucial to you, look for similar statistics that help verify it or find out as much as you can about the methodology, sponsorship, sample size, etc., of the survey or study that produced it.

Apply your own common sense to it

Later, after you have collected all possible data, apply your own common sense to it. Does something sound too good to be true? Is this fantastic data coming from only one source? Does the publisher of the data have a vested interest? If so, don't necessarily throw the item out, but don't bet the farm on it, either.

Decide whether you have enough data to make a decision

Go back to the lists of questions you wrote on Worksheet 2 and made in chapter 2. Have you found the answers to all the questions that can be answered by secondary data? If not, keep going. Has the data you found led to new questions? Then keep going. As you find more data, apply the same three tests you've been applying: verify, use your common sense, and ask whether you've got enough.

Taking a little extra time and care should help assure you sound data from which to generate good information and an excellent marketing strategy. Remember, no matter what else you do, you're already ahead of your competitors who aren't doing any market research. Go back to your lists of questions from chapter 2; now use Worksheet 3 to decide what kind of secondary data would supply the answers to your questions. Check off the categories of data you will need. Use the blanks to elaborate. Don't be limited by our categories. There's room to add more of your own. If you require a piece of business data, it's probably out there. Remember, some of your questions cannot be answered by secondary data and will require primary data instead.

Sample 3 shows what secondary data Clarice decided she would need to answer her questions.

WORKSHEET 3
WHAT SECONDARY DATA DO YOU NEED?

Categories of Secondary Data

Check the categories of secondary data that you might need. Use the blanks to elaborate. Don't be limited by our categories. There's room to add your own at the bottom. Remember, all the information you need may not come from secondary sources.

- ☐ Demographic statistics: ____________________
- ☐ Scientific study data: ____________________
- ☐ Media survey data: ____________________
- ☐ Public polls: ____________________
- ☐ Patent and trademark information: ____________________
- ☐ Legal information: ____________________
- ☐ Addresses and phone numbers: ____________________
- ☐ Information on business procedures: ____________________
- ☐ Prices and specifications: ____________________
- ☐ Other: ____________________
- ☐ Other: ____________________
- ☐ Other: ____________________

Case Study

In order to fill out Worksheet 3, Clarice goes back to the sheet she filled out after her brainstorming session (see Sample 2) and asks herself, "Where am I most likely to find the answers to my questions?"

Since many of her questions concern the makeup of her target market, she knows she will need several good sources of demographic data, starting with national and regional census reports. She needs psychographic data, too, and she can find some in media surveys and public opinion polls (though she knows much of this will also have to come from primary data — her own surveys of potential customers).

The nature of her product allows her to bypass scientific studies, and although she will certainly need some legal advice before setting up her marketing venture, she doesn't think she needs to look up any specific legal data such as zoning laws or tax codes. She definitely wants to find addresses and phone numbers of business associations that can help her market her product, so she checks off that category. Then, in case her research shows her that direct mail is her best marketing method, she adds mailing list sources to the things she wants to look for.

She knows she needs information on business procedures. Some of that will come from library books; more will come from those associations whose addresses she's going to seek. Still more may come from small business advisers in her own community.

Finally, she decides to look up prices and specifications of magazine and newspaper ads. Having this information will help her decide whether or not to advertise in those media.

She can't think of anything else at the moment, but she knows she will think of other questions and stumble on other sources of information as she conducts her research.

SAMPLE 3
WHAT SECONDARY DATA DO YOU NEED?

Categories of Secondary Data

Check the categories of secondary data that you might need. Use the blanks to elaborate. Don't be limited by our categories. There's room to add your own at the bottom. Remember, all the information you need may not come from secondary sources.

- [x] Demographic statistics: Executive and other upscale women/local/regional/national; other upscale people
- [ ] Scientific study data: ________
- [x] Media survey data: (If I decide to place ads in magazines) — who reads the publication; which sections are most read?
- [x] Public polls: (Maybe?) Buying habits of my target
- [x] Patent and trademark information: Look for competing products; similar graphics
- [ ] Legal information: ________
- [x] Addresses and phone numbers: Media; marketing and business associations; mailing list sources (later?)
- [x] Information on business procedures: Direct marketing resources and techniques
- [x] Prices and specifications: Media ad prices (magazines/local newspaper); information on mailing costs and methods
- [ ] Other: ________
- [ ] Other: ________
- [ ] Other: ________

Chapter 5
FINDING THE SECONDARY DATA YOU NEED

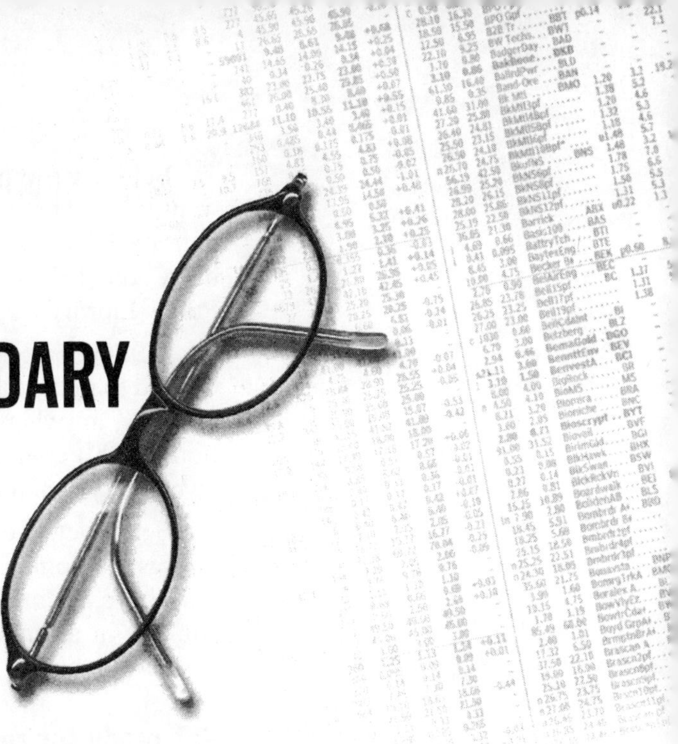

Now that you know what you're looking for, you may be able to get most of the secondary data you need in a single morning. You'll make three or four stops:

(a) Your local library

(b) The chamber of commerce

(c) The Economic Development Administration (EDA) or regional development board

(d) Your local community college business development center

(e) Business Development Bank of Canada (BDC)

Some other places to investigate at your leisure include the following:

(a) Local media (for survey data)

(b) Local offices of trade associations

(c) Consulates and embassies (for import and export information)

(d) College or university libraries

> *The world's biggest consulting firm charges nothing and probably has a branch in your town. It's called the library.*
>
> INC., JULY, 1992

THE LIBRARY

As writers, we spend a lot of time doing research. But we never cease to be amazed at the amount of business information we can get during a single stop at the library.

Before writing this chapter, we did just what you will do. We went to the library and spent a few hours tracking down secondary data for business. We made stops at the Aberdeen Timberland Library, the Prince George Public Library, and the Pierce County Public Library.

We deliberately stayed away from large-city libraries because we wanted to make the point that this kind of data is available to nearly anybody, anywhere. Even our smallest library (Aberdeen, population 15,000) contained enough reference books to keep a business owner very well informed.

Better yet, even the smallest library is usually linked to other libraries via computer, including the Internet, and many small systems have a central reference desk reachable by a 1-800 number. If you live in a major city, you simply have an even bigger treasure trove available.

Get ready for research

Most reference information is in noncirculating books, so take a notebook, a pen, and cash for the copier. Plan to do most of your work on the premises. Many libraries also have a quick reference phone line, so you could call ahead to get a general idea of what the library can offer you.

Take your worksheets, questions, and notes with you so you can make sure not to forget to look up anything.

Your friendly reference librarian

Your single best first step is to find a good research librarian and buy him or her lunch. It's the librarians's job to help find answers, and they love to do it.

David Thornburg,
Director of the Small Business Development Center at the Wharton School of Business
Inc., July, 1992

The first thing to do when you arrive at the library is stop at the reference desk and tell the librarian what kind of information you're looking for. Bypass the book catalogue for now; it contains too many listings with too little detail and may lead you down blind alleys. The librarian can usually guide you straight to the information you need.

If you aren't a frequent user of the reference desk, you may be hesitant to bother the librarian or afraid to ask dumb questions. You needn't be. Librarians are unfailingly helpful and they live for the challenge of tracking down information. Go for it!

Most Canadian libraries will have a good supply of both Canadian and US references. US libraries, depending on their size and location, will also have a selection of Canadian reference books.

Libraries in both nations are increasingly carrying an ever-larger selection of resources to assist businesses doing business with Europe and Asia.

While it is impossible to list all the source materials you can find at your library, Appendix 1 gives a sampling of the kinds of useful publications that are available.

Computer databases

Most library reference departments also have computer databases containing millions of additional statistics. A database is nothing more than a compilation of data. It can be easier than using a book once you know how. There should be written instructions available. But once again the rule is, If you don't know how, ask the librarian.

What kind of data can you expect to find? The most common databases contain —

(a) lists of publications and articles (similar to the printed *Readers Guide to Periodical Literature*); and

(b) abstracts of articles that have appeared in scientific, medical, and other professional literature.

Others supply you with data on population characteristics, manufacturing statistics, health statistics, the arts, social trends, and a host of other subjects.

Databases come in two different forms: CD-ROM and online. CD-ROM databases have information stored on compact disks. You choose the disks you need, insert them into the library's computer, and conduct your search. You will probably be allowed to use them exactly as you would any other research material.

Online databases don't physically reside at the library. Rather, you use the library's computer to access other computers containing the data you need. Online databases may be reserved for the librarian's use, or you may be charged to use them.

Some on-line services are set up to search multiple databases at once, cross-checking between them. You simply define the parameters of your search (specifying something like *the ten US metro areas with the lowest tax rates, peak years for lumber production in Alberta,* or *number of households on Prince Edward Island headed by single women*) and the computer conducts the search and presents you with the information.

If you own a computer with a modem, you can also subscribe to many of these same online databases. If you own a computer equipped with a CD-ROM drive, you can buy your own CD-ROM library. But for a one-time research project, your best course is probably to stick with the library.

Circulating books

More help is available in the form of circulating books, those you can take back to your home or office. Once again, even a small library will have (or have access to) enormous numbers of books. In the smallest of our three libraries, for example, we found an entire small-business resource center containing hundreds of books on advertising, marketing, starting a small business, hiring employees, writing business plans, and much, much more.

Now's the time to check out that main catalogue you bypassed earlier. Most libraries today have computerized their catalogues, making them much faster and simpler to use. Where there used to be separate catalogues for author, title, and subject, there's now one computerized catalogue that covers them all.

Not only can you tell the computer to search for various titles, subjects, or authors, but you can also limit your search in various ways. You might, for example, be able to specify French language books only, or those books containing the words *marketing* and *export* and *Japan* in their subject descriptions. You can also print the catalogue information, then carry the computer printout to the shelves. No more writing Dewey decimal numbers on scraps of paper!

Try the library's main catalogue under these categories:

(a) Accounting/bookkeeping

(b) Advertising

(c) Associations

(d) Business

(e) Computer

(f) Consumer

(g) Demographics

(h) Distribution

(i) Finance

(j) Forecasting

(k) Importing/exporting

(l) Management
(m) Market research
(n) Marketing
(o) Marketplaces
(p) Meetings
(q) Office management
(r) Positioning
(s) Presentations
(t) Retail
(u) Sales/selling
(v) Tax/taxation
(w) Trade shows
(x) Video

Many of these topics are covered by other titles in the Self-Counsel Series.

NEXT STOPS: THE CHAMBER OF COMMERCE AND THE EDA

After a couple of hours at the library, head for the chamber of commerce and the Economic Development Administration (EDA) or regional development board. In our experience, you'll often find them in the same building.

Much of the local community information you will find in the library will have been generated and supplied by the local chamber and the EDA, often in conjunction with a government regional planning commission. You will find additional and more specific information by going straight to the source.

Types of help the chamber can offer

The chamber of commerce can give you general information about the community and its businesses, and put you in contact with other business people. The chamber's "Ambassadors" program (while admittedly a tool for recruiting new chamber members) helps pair experienced business people with newcomers. The experienced business people are usually more than happy to act as mentors to aspiring new business people. Ask for their advice.

Types of help the EDA can offer

The EDA or regional development board can give you more specific information and advice. While the chamber exists to help businesses and the community in general, the EDA's mandate is to help businesses individually. The EDA can offer —

(a) advice on financing sources;

(b) locations, rates, and zoning information for local industrial parks and buildings;

(c) utility and transportation rates;

(d) statistics on the community and its business conditions;

(e) contacts and advice on dealing with local government agencies; and

(f) knowledge about local regulations and environmental conditions.

> *An expert is a [person] who has made all the mistakes which can be made in a very narrow field.*
>
> NIELS BOHR

THE BUSINESS DEVELOPMENT CENTER

Your community college small-business development center or local office of the BDC (in Canada) can offer you the most hands-on assistance of any of the other stops you make on your morning of research.

Experts at the center can help you —

(a) find sources for financing and fill out the paperwork to get loans,

(b) draw up a business plan,

(c) find outlets for your product,

(d) establish a bookkeeping system, and

(e) plan your advertising and marketing.

> Randy Mahaffey, CEO of Plymart, a siding, windows, and trim supplying firm in Georgia, used a local professor of marketing for market research. The college professor designed a customer survey for Plymart, which had been doing $45 million per year. After following through on some of the ideas suggested in the survey, the results were a whopping 22 percent increase in sales. The cost was minimal. Mahaffey happily declared, "For less than $5,000, we got $100,000 worth of information."
>
> *INC., NOVEMBER, 1992*

The center may also be able to put you in touch with a professor, teacher, or other expert who can give you additional one-on-one assistance. In short, the center can guide you through just about every step of establishing your business or marketing your new product or service. They can even guide you through the rest of your marketing research. Of course, it will take more than a morning to get all this planning done! But it will only take a few minutes to stop in or call to find out how the people at the center can help you.

There can be a lot of overlap between the services provided by the chamber, the EDA, and the business development center. If there is no community college in your city, you may find the same kind of help at the EDA or chamber. In areas without an EDA, the chamber or the community college may perform the same function.

Wherever you must go to get it, however, all of the above types of advice and information are available and the vast majority of it is either very low in cost or free.

WHAT QUESTIONS HAVE YOU ANSWERED?

Now, go back to Worksheet 2 in chapter 3. How many of your questions did you answer in your morning's research? How many others arose as a result of the research?

You may find that your questions are becoming more and more specific as you go. For instance, you may have started off with a question like, Are there enough members of the target market to make my business worthwhile? If your data told you there were, you probably started asking yourself questions such as, In what area of town do these people do most of their shopping? or How much would they pay for my deluxe model widget?

Check off the questions in Worksheet 2 that you have gotten satisfactory answers to. Use Worksheet 4 to record your new questions, whether they can be answered by secondary or primary data sources, and what possible methods you might use to obtain that data (surveys, library research, etc.).

If your new questions can be answered by secondary research, go back to the library, the Internet, the chamber, or the EDA until you've found all the data you need.

Now use Worksheet 5 to list the key data you've found so far that help prove or disprove your hypothesis. If you're typical, you'll still have a long way to go before completely proving the hypothesis, but you've probably found some important indicators of whether you're on the right road. Revise your hypothesis if you need to. We'll come back and check it once again after you finish your primary research.

Samples 4 and 5 show how Clarice completed these worksheets.

Case Study

Clarice Rogers returned from her morning's research with a legal pad filled with notes, 30 or 40 photocopies of book and magazine pages, as well as a several-inches-thick stack of literature from the chamber and EDA.

After sorting through it all, she had the answer to one very big question: Are there enough target customers for me to market locally? Census data and reports from the EDA had shown her there were not. To successfully market her appointment calendar, she would have to reach outside the local market.

However, economic trend data, magazine articles on consumer buying trends, and articles on executive styles had given her a more positive answer to another question: Are executive women truly my market? Economic data and consumer trend articles indicated that upscale people were continuing to buy small luxury items despite a general economic downturn. Articles on the lifestyles of executive women said that these women were increasingly willing to express their feminine side in the office. Since Clarice's book was a delicate work of art as well as a useful executive tool, she felt very encouraged.

Checking her hypothesis, she found it to be still sound but far from proven. She had also found, in directories of manufacturers and in magazine ads, a little information on competitors and their products. She made a note to write for more information about these.

WORKSHEET 4
ADDITIONAL QUESTIONS ARISING FROM YOUR RESEARCH

List what new questions about your project need to be answered. What kind of data, primary or secondary, might answer your additonal questions. What method (survey, poll, library research, etc.) will you use to gather this data.

	Additional Questions	Primary Data	Secondary Data	Possible Method
1.				
2.				
3.				
4.				
5.				
6.				
7.				
8.				
9.				
10.				

WORKSHEET 5
CHECKING YOUR HYPOTHESIS

The hypothesis to check is: ____

____

____

	Key Findings From Your Research
1.	
2.	
3.	
4.	
5.	
6.	

Hypothesis Summary

1. Is your hypothesis still valid? Yes_______ No_______
2. If yes, are there still parts of it to be researched further? Yes_______ No _______
3. If no, do you want to:
   a) Rewrite or refine your hypothesis? Yes_______ No _______
   b) Gather more information? Yes_______ No_______
   c) Abandon the project? Yes_______ No _______
4. My new hypothesis is: ____

____

____

If your hypothesis still has elements that need to be supported or disproved, or if you have rewritten your hypothesis, you need to gather more information.

SAMPLE 4
ADDITIONAL QUESTIONS ARISING FROM YOUR RESEARCH

List what new questions about your project need to be answered. What kind of data, primary or secondary, might answer your additonal questions. What method (survey, poll, library research, etc.) will you use to gather this data.

	Additional Questions	Primary Data	Secondary Data	Possible Method
1.	Is direct mail my best marketing method?	X	X	a) Check list directories b) Poll potential buyers
2.	What are the best mailing list sources?		X	Check directories
3.	Are there other competitors I'm not aware of?		X	Manufacturers and publisher directories
4.	Best packaging, mailing methods?	X	X	a) Check directories for packaging companies b) Call suppliers
5.	Can I confirm my secondary buying trends among executive women?	X		Survey
6.				
7.				
8.				
9.				
10.				

SAMPLE 5
CHECKING YOUR HYPOTHESIS

The hypothesis to check is: This product will be used by executives and other upscale women and will be purchased by them for their own use as gifts.

	Key Findings From Your Research
1.	There are not enough high-income women in my area for me to market locally
2.	Magazine advertising — national, anyway — is probably too expensive
3.	Executive women are my best market
4.	I have few competitors
5.	
6.	

Hypothesis Summary

1. Is your hypothesis still valid? Yes X No _______
2. If yes, are there still parts of it to be researched further? Yes X No _______
3. If no, do you want to:
   a) Rewrite or refine your hypothesis? Yes _______ No _______
   b) Gather more information? Yes _______ No _______
   c) Abandon the project? Yes _______ No _______
4. My new hypothesis is: ______________________________

If your hypothesis still has elements that need to be supported or disproved, or if you have rewritten your hypothesis, you need to gather more information.

Chapter 6
PRIMARY DATA: YOU'RE ALREADY SURROUNDED BY IT

If the basic purpose of your research project was market analysis, it's possible that, once you've finished your secondary research, you've finished your research, period. But since you undoubtedly have other goals, like finding out how potential customers will respond to your specific product, service, or advertising, it's time to move on to primary research — generating data for yourself.

THE INFORMATION YOU MAY ALREADY HAVE

In the previous chapter, we showed you how to find data someone else generated. All you had to do was go get it. For the rest of the book, we talk about data you generate about your own business and its customers.

> *People are usually more convinced by reasons they discovered themselves than by those found by others.*
>
> Blaise Pascal

To get some of this, you'll need to conduct surveys. But a lot of what you need may be right in front of your nose, and you just may not think of it as data. You may regard it simply as instinct, common knowledge, everyday assumptions, or even gossip. But if you can use it in your business, it's data.

Here are some sources you may already have about those all-important people, your customers:

(a) Customer service inquiries

(b) Your own salespeople and prospects

(c) Coffee breaks

(d) Trade journals
(e) Service and professional organizations
(f) Special promotions
(g) Complaints
(h) Visitor log records for Web sites

> Deck House, a home building company in Massachusetts, dedicated an 800 line for customer service. In the first year, they received 2,018 calls. Once service reps had answered customers' questions, they asked a few of their own. From these informal surveys, Deck House learned how design preferences varied from state to state, and that information helped them satisfy their customers. About 25 percent of the callers were also willing to give Deck House names of friends they thought would be interested in receiving sales literature.
>
> *Inc.*, November, 1992

Customer service inquiries

Keep a record of the kinds of questions people ask about your product or service. You'll learn a lot about what they want, need, and expect from you. While you have customers on the phone, at your desk, or at your counter you can also take the opportunity to ask for information about themselves and their perceptions of your company.

Salespeople and sales contacts

Listen to your salespeople (or to your prospects if you are the one doing the sales calls). What do prospects say, or how do they react? "I could tell they were going to buy even before I showed it to them." "Younger people don't want to listen to the benefits." "You know, when I mention 'quality,' their eyes seem to glaze over." "I'm embarrassed when I mention the price." "People touch the surface, then walk away."

Ask your salespeople to repeat dialogues they have with prospects (or recall them yourself). What did you or the salesperson say? What did the customer say? Get a flavor for the entire conversation, not just a chance phrase. Put yourself into the customer's shoes and mentally walk around your product, metaphorically kicking its tires.

Coffee breaks

Breaks are fun. People talk about their favorite sitcom on TV, the latest movie they saw, events with their friends and family ... and work. In a relaxed atmosphere, you can discover many truths. Don't press, just relax and laugh along with your partners or coworkers. Listen and remember. "My next-door neighbor, Jack, says that he'd stop and try our new sandwich, but every time he drives by, the lines are too long." "My grandmother won't buy anything that comes in a six-pack." "I tried that new line of wax we're carrying. It works better than shoe polish." All this is grist for your information mill.

Trade journals

Trade publications arrive so often when you're in business that you probably won't read them all. But you should. At least skim through them, mark interesting or useful passages, and tear articles out for your "good idea" file. Don't overlook what others in your industry are saying about their customers. Remember, they're your customers, too.

Yes, we know we're cheating. This is really good old secondary data, covered in chapters 4 and 5. But since it pertains specifically to *your* customers and *your* field and keeps coming in long after your day at the library is over, we thought it was a good idea to mention it again.

Service and professional organizations

Organizations like Rotary and Kiwanis, and professional groups like Sales and Marketing Executives, Women Independent Business Owners, or the International Association of Business Communicators can be very valuable. They not only give you great business contacts, they can present you with informal opportunities to discuss your product or service among peers. "Do you think I should add electronic toys to my product line?" "Drop in and I'll give you a free treatment." "I notice you tried the new computerized vending machine the other day. Did you think it was easy to operate?"

Special promotions

Daily, weekly, or other specials can give you the opportunity to test demand for products or services. Printers may offer free colored inks on different days, then see which color draws the most customers. Restaurants offer lunch specials. Car dealers have "one only" sales, offering a specific kind of car to test how many potential buyers respond. Such specials generate information and an opportunity for business. Have you kept track of how many people ask for your specials? This is data; don't waste it.

Simply Sally's, a health food restaurant in Manitoba, has a clientele that enjoys trying new dishes. So Sally tests potential menu items by introducing them as daily specials. After serving cheese tortellini vinaigrette on 12 successive Fridays, Sally determined that the response was high enough to merit including the dish on her regular menu. On the other hand, the tofu bean soup special, while well liked by a few, didn't draw enough response to become an everyday item.

Complaints

There's nothing worse than a dissatisfied customer, unless it's failing to learn from a dissatisfied customer. There's a wealth of information to be found in complaints. "The handle feels awkward." "How come it only comes in blue?" "Don't you have one with more padding?" "Well, how long is it supposed to last?" While a few isolated complaints may mean nothing more than human nature in action, similar complaints coming from different people present valuable opportunities for learning.

Visitor log records for Web sites

Some Web sites have software that record the IP address of visitors. Armed with an IP address, you can generally see what companies are visiting your site or your competitor's Web site.

IN-HOUSE RESOURCES FOR MARKETING SURVEYS

When you do need to conduct surveys, you can make the job easier and cheaper by having an existing list or database of your customers and prospects. This list gives you a built-in sample group for your survey and it can also be used for your advertising mailings. The bigger the mailing list you have, the more opportunity you will have to make your research and your marketing productive.

You should try to get the name, address, and phone number of every possible customer and prospect and continually add the information to your customer list. Regularly record new names in your database. It's easier if your list is computerized, but even a box of index cards will do. These names will come in handy time and again for many reasons.

There are a number of simple ways to collect names:

(a) At point of sale

(b) By having a mailing-list sign-up

(c) From business cards

(d) From sales receipts, invoices, order forms, and applications

If you run a retail business, conduct a drawing for merchandise or a gift certificate. Ask customers to place their business card or a slip of paper with their name, address, and phone number on it in a fish bowl on your counter. You can also ask customers to sign up to receive mailings from you, such as a newsletter or notification of sales.

Ask fellow members of Rotary, Toastmasters, Soroptimist, etc., for their business cards. Ask for cards of members of your professional groups, too, if they fit your target. Also collect the business cards people give you in the course of a normal day.

Record the names of people who buy from you or apply for your services (being careful to respect any confidentiality agreements, of course).

> *Profit: Information Technology for Entrepreneurs* is a professional trade journal offered free to qualified individuals. To qualify, readers must complete a questionnaire asking for information such as whether the reader has the authority to purchase new equipment and what computer hardware and software the reader's company plans to purchase. *Profit* uses this information to help select article topics and to market their magazine to advertisers, who pay for the privilege of reaching highly qualified potential customers.

HOW TO USE THE DATA YOU ALREADY HAVE

To begin to use the data you have in hand, use Worksheet 6 to write down everything you already know about your customers, their needs, their wants, their expectations, and their perceptions of your business. Use the worksheet as a thought-starter, but feel free to take pages and pages to write down other thoughts you've had and comments you've heard. Later, this data will help you ask the most meaningful questions on your surveys and make the most market-satisfying business plans.

You may be confident you already know the answers to the questions on the worksheet. But by really thinking about the answers and writing them down, you will discover things you didn't know and you'll make connections you never made before. You'll deepen your knowledge and come to understand how something that happens during a coffee break relates to something that occurs during a call on a client or customer.

By showing you where your greatest dilemmas are, or in what areas your existing knowledge is weak or strong, your answers will also help you decide what to put on your market research questionnaires.

WHAT YOU ALREADY KNOW (OR CAN EASILY LEARN) ABOUT YOUR COMPETITION

Who is your competition? How well liked are they? How strong are they? What is their future? Just as you already have many answers about your own business, you also have, or can easily get, data about your competitors and potential competitors.

> *Ask questions. Don't be shy or polite. It's your future.*
>
> LAUREN KARPINSKI

Here are some everyday sources of information on competitors:

(a) Customers, other competitors, and suppliers

(b) Networking groups

(c) Newsletters

(d) Annual reports and sales literature

(e) The newspaper and other publications

(f) The Internet

(g) Yourself

WORKSHEET 6
WHAT YOU ALREADY KNOW ABOUT YOUR BUSINESS

Write down what you know about your customers, their needs, their wants, their expectations, and their perceptions of your business by answering the following questions. Feel free to use additional sheets of paper.

1. What kind of comments have I heard from customers and/or salespeople?

a. Positive comments

____

____

____

b. Negative comments

____

____

____

2. Is there anything people have been consistently asking for that I could supply?

____

____

____

3. Is there a pattern to the complaints or service inquiries I've been receiving?

Yes _____ No _____

4. If yes, what can I do to fill the need?

____

____

____

5. What have I heard around the office from employees or partners (from family members and friends if you are a one-person operation)?

____

____

____

6. What articles have I seen recently in trade journals or other publications that I thought had meaning for my business?

____

____

____

WORKSHEET 6 — Continued

7. What have I learned from organizations I belong to? Are there people in the organizations who can help me? Literature, classes, or other assistance?

____

____

____

8. What have I learned from special events, promotions, or sales I've had in the past?

a. Successful promotions

____

____

____

b. Less successful promotions

____

____

____

9. Which seasons, days of the week, or times of day have been best for my business, and why?

____

____

____

10. Are there problems customers or employess may not be expressing? If so, how can I learn more about them and improve my product or service as a result?

____

____

____

Now take some time to consider how you can best capitalize on your successes, failures, and general knowledge you already have about your business.

Customers, other competitors, and suppliers

All these have one thing in common: they're all interested in talking about your competition. When a customer says, "I just won't deal with Competitor X any more; they were so rude to me when I tried to return something I'd bought," or a supplier says, "Yeah, Competitor Z just ordered 500 of those in blue, " don't think of it as gossip, think of it as data.

Networking groups

In the same way groups and associations can give you data about your own business, they can provide great forums for finding out who your competition is, what they're doing, and how they are perceived.

Newsletters

Do any of your competitors publish newsletters? Get on the mailing list (even if you have to do it in a friend's name). Newsletters are filled with information about competitors' new product lines or services, new employees, locations, advertising, and more. In addition, they can give you a good sense of your competitors' personal style. Are they formal, casual, friendly, professional, good-humored, staid? All this can help you decide how to focus both your research and your competitive efforts.

Annual reports and sales literature

If a competitor publishes an annual report, you can mine it for information about the company's financial health and philosophy (keep your bull detector operating, though!). Competitors' sales literature can also give you a wealth of information about the way they do business, and give you ammo for both market research questions and competitive strategies.

The newspaper and other publications

Any time you see a news item about a competitor, clip it out. If they've hired a new employee, acquired a big contract, been accused of polluting, you'll want to know. Also keep an eye on their advertising and analyze it. Do they put a heavy emphasis on price? If so, can you compete with them? Are their ads professional looking? Do they attract the eye? Is their advertising so consistent that you can tell their ads from anyone else's at a glance? Knowing all this will help you craft, and test, your own advertising.

The Internet

With the Internet you can view your competitors' Web sites and check out their prices, services, product lines, guarantees, and even customer service issues.

Searches using your competitor's name may yield results in chatrooms, news groups, and other references from a wide variety of sources.

Yourself

Once again, don't overlook the obvious. What have *you* observed about your competitors? Have you called them on the phone to enquire about prices and services? Have you talked with their salespeople? Examined their products? Browsed through their stores? Received their sales literature? What did you learn? What did you observe?

Sit down right now and ask yourself what you already know about your competition. Using Worksheet 7, write down everything you can think of that applies to *all* your competitors. Write down even the smallest things, even things that "everyone knows" or that you simply take for granted. Things like, they all carry similar product lines; none is marketing to homemakers; or, all are run by men.

Now make copies of Worksheet 8 and fill one out for each competitor. Write down everything you can think of about each one of them. Put a star at the top of the sheets that carry information about your biggest competitors, and spend extra time thinking and writing comments about those businesses. Again, no thought is too small or unimportant to write down. *Highest prices, Owner dresses sloppily, Great location, They had tax trouble three years ago, or Specialize in Guess? sportswear*— these are the kind of comments you'll want to write down.

As you did when you wrote information about your own company, feel free to take as many extra pages as you need.

Take all the comments you wrote about your own business and put them in a file labeled US. Take all the comments you wrote about your competition and put them in a file labeled THEM.

As you go about your daily business, look and listen for any other information that comes your way. Write it down, clip it out, save it, and put it in the appropriate file. These files will help you when it comes time to write your market research questionnaires. And they'll also help you in the days, weeks, months, and years of competition ahead.

WORKSHEET 7
YOUR COMPETITION

List what you know about your competition.

	What I know about my competition
1.	
2.	
3.	
4.	
5.	
6.	
7.	
8.	
9.	
10.	
11.	
12.	

WORKSHEET 8
YOUR COMPETITORS

Competitor: ______________________________

List what you know about this competitor.

	What I know about this competitor
1.	
2.	
3.	
4.	
5.	
6.	
7.	
8.	
9.	
10.	
11.	
12.	

Case Study

Entering a new field, Clarice Rogers has had little opportunity to pick up daily data. Her US and THEM folders are very slim to begin with. Yet even she has a surprising amount of information about the market for her appointment book.

Recalling comments of customers, friends, and craft-show competitors and customers, she writes:

"I'd pay $50 for something like that."

"There are a lot of nice appointment calendars out there, but I've never seen anything as elegant as yours."

"You'd need to bind it with something more durable than that fabric."

"I'd pay $35 or $40 for something like that, even though that's an awful lot for an appointment book."

"Would you make it in different colors?"

"You should try putting an ad for it in *Lears* magazine. Or maybe *Working Woman*."

"The packaging is going to make a big difference in what you can charge for it."

These and other comments she placed in her US file.

Then, to start her THEM file, she visited elegant stationery, leather, department, and card stores, looking for unusual and expensive appointment books. Whenever she found a comparable product, she made notes on its price, quality, materials, packaging, and other features.

She also made careful note of the fact that she didn't find a single book as elegant as the one she planned to manufacture. She added two questions to the note: *Is this a plus — my product is unique? Or is this a minus — there is no demand for a book like mine?*

She wrote to three of the manufacturers she'd found in a directory, asking for information on their product lines (telling them only that she was planning to go into business dealing in these items, not revealing that she was considering competing with them). She also responded to one of the magazine ads she'd copied, sending $29.95 to order a competitor's appointment book. While this was a lot to pay for an appointment book, she thought, it was a very small amount to pay for market research. Spending $29.95 now could keep her from wasting $39,000 later.

Chapter 7

INTERNET MARKET RESEARCH

HOW TO SEARCH FOR INFORMATION

Market research on the Internet is wonderful. You can find just about any information or data if you know where and how to look for it. But in order to find out information you must first know how to use directories, search engines, pay-per-click search engines, and other sources of information.

A *directory* is a listing of various Web sites in clear-cut categories. Yahoo is a directory. It's probably the most popular search site on the Internet, even though it is not a search engine. The problem with Yahoo and other directories is that you only see what that particular directory wants you to see. Not everyone gets listed in a directory. Directories like Yahoo charge a fee to be listed, which can limit search results.

A *search engine* is just that — an engine or program that searches for information based on the criteria you give it. For example, you are going to visit Portland, Oregon, and you want to find a restaurant with a meeting room. You would conduct a general search for: *Portland restaurant meeting rooms*. The results from the search engine would contain information submitted to the search engine from various Portland restaurants. Companies, and individuals submit their Web sites to search engines to be listed on them. If the submitted Web site meets certain requirements, then it will be listed. The problem with search engines is that their number is shrinking as more and more search engine companies consolidate and search for revenue.

Pay-per-click search engines are a hybrid of the directory and the search engine. Three of the most popular are Overture, Findwhat, and Kanoodle. Generally, if you visit a pay-per-click search engine, you are going to see a list of sites that paid for their placement in search results. For example, if you are searching for knit caps on a pay-per-click search engine, you will be shown a list of sites that feature knit caps, but the top listings will be given to those who pay the most. Some pay-per-click search engines provide their list of paid advertisers first and then list sites from a built-in search engine. So, you get limited results based on a fee-based structure for placement and then a list of other sites.

As search engines and directories look for ways to bring in revenue, they turn to the pay-per-clicks and become affiliates of pay-per-clicks. To the untrained eye, a search engine might look like it's bringing you focused results, but really what some search engines and directories now deliver is a combination of paid results from various pay-per-click search engines, their own advertisers, and a few search results to fill out the page.

A search begins by entering keywords. In the example above, the search is for knit caps. If you merely entered the words knit caps, you might get sites that feature knit caps. You also might find results for phrases that somehow contain knit caps or a combination of knit caps with other words. You might find a site that features information on presentation graphics with part of the description including *titles all in caps*. The more focused search would start off with the use of quotation marks. "Knit Caps" will give you results for knit caps only. Sometimes you will need to search with both quotation marks and without. You might get some of the same results, but you should get a wider variety using both methods.

Our three favorite places to find market research data are Altavista, Google, and eBay — two search engines and an auction site.

Altavista used to have the largest database of Internet sites. It might still have the largest database but it's not the most popular. Google is the number-one search engine by usage. We like the layout of both search engines as well as the number and quality of results. Google is the search engine of choice on Yahoo. As we said earlier, Yahoo is a directory, but they also have a search engine on their site, which is powered by Google.

By using eBay you can find both new products and used products in your searches. And, since eBay has grown to be so huge, you can find almost anything listed for sale there — even advertising.

PUTTING YOUR SEARCHES TO WORK

Okay, you've developed a product or you've found a product that you can represent. Using the Internet, what can you find out about your business possibilities?

Product research

Use the search engines for general information. Look at every single page for the first couple hundred results or until you stop seeing anything relevant. Sometimes a search engine will deliver thousands and thousands of results. As you weed through them, you will begin to notice that the pages you are looking at may contain some of the words in your search, but they no longer contain real information concerning your actual search. For example, if you are searching for chocolate covered candy, and after reviewing a number of sites that offer information on chocolate covered candy you start finding sites that refer to exotic dancers named Candy, you should stop your search and redefine your search terms.

Write down notes about anything interesting you see. Each site you visit may give you ideas about your product or about your Web site. For instance, you might find an interesting color combination that works with your product, or an interactive program that might work for your Web site. This is market research brainstorming. You don't need one right answer because there is always more than one right answer. You're looking for information — raw data. Use this as an idea generator concerning your product for marketing, presentation, format, sizes, applications, etc.

Make a list of your competitors and visit their Web sites. A Web site reveals a considerable amount of information concerning the operation of a business.

Start an information sheet concerning your known competition's Web sites. You should consider the following questions:

- What features do you like?
- Do they have an *About Us* section?
- Do they have any statistics available? (Check their counter if they have one to see how many people are visiting their site.)

Compare features

Make a page with two columns: We have/They have.

- Are there other products like yours?
- If there are no products exactly the same, are there products that are similar?
- If there are similar products, what price are they selling them for?
- Would your product be an improvement? If so, how?
- Visit chatrooms and look for comments, complaints, and suggestions about the site and its products.

Distribution

- What kind of distribution is working for them? (i.e., United Parcel Service, Federal Express, postal express)
- Do you see any problems with your competition's distribution?
- How are others selling similar products? (In stores? As seen on TV? Exclusively from their Web site?)
- Who manufactures or supplies similar products?

Competition

- What competitors can you discover on the Internet that you didn't know about?
- Who are the key people involved in the competition?
- How successful are your competitors?
- How are your competitors marketing their products? (i.e., "Look for our ads … ")
- Does your competitor have paid advertising? (Banners? Display ads? Text links?)
- Who endorses your competitor's product?
- Who links to your competitor's Web site?
- How good are your competitors' Web sites?
- Have any celebrities mentioned this product?
- Are there any comments or testimonials concerning this product?
- Are there Web sites that have noncompetitive but similar products?

Don Doman has a leadership/management training product Web site and has searched the net for suppliers of products he would like to sell on his site. Finding a unique product, he sent an e-mail asking about the possibility of listing their product on his site. Receiving no response, he thought about their product and within 48 hours he had a similar product at a fraction of the cost. Their product is no longer unique — and he added some improvements.

- Do they have links?
- Could you write them and ask if they would give you a reciprocal link?
- Could they offer your product for sale in addition to their own?
- Could you offer their product as well as your own on your site?
- Could you market your product on other sites?

Name and domain address

- What are you going to call your product?
- What are you going to call your company?
- What domain addresses are available?
- What keyword inhabited domain names are available? (For instance, if you are selling western red cedar burled knife handles you may want to have a URL of <www.burled-knife-handles.com>, <www.wooden-knife-handles.com>, or <www.western-red-cedar-knives.com>.)
- Are there any possible trademark or copyright infringements hiding in the bushes? Check it out. (Search for trademark or copyright registration.)

JavaScript

- Does the site use JavaScript? JavaScript is a computer program that works within Web sites. For instance, a JavaScript application could let someone visiting your site send the address to a friend. They might click on a button that says, "Share this site with a friend." Once they click on the button, they can enter the information concerning the site and e-mail it to a friend.
- Who supplies the JavaScript? If you see an attractive idea on another Web site, you might be able to lift it. Many times JavaScripts can be used in a cut-and-paste manner. Sometimes you can use JavaScript as shareware and all you need to do is give appropriate credit to the originator of the program. You will find that sometimes JavaScripts are free, and other times you may need to pay for them.
- Can you use their JavaScript on your site? You may need to obtain permission. You may also need to upload other script elements to your Web site to make it compatible.

- Why does the JavaScript seem to be useful? Ask yourself what you like about the script and what it does for the site.
- Does the JavaScript make the site interesting?
- Does it improve the Web site's look or functionality?

After you've gathered all of your information, you're ready to use it in conjunction with other strategies mentioned throughout this book.

Industrial espionage has been big business for a long time. Basically, the more you know about your competition — their efforts and their strategies — the better prepared you'll be to compete with them. There are software programs on the market you can use to find out about your competition's traffic, links, and visitors. You can locate them via searches for "traffic analysis software," "spy software," and "your competition." You will need to purchase the software to use it, but some will offer you a download demo to try it out.

There are also free sites on the Internet that can tell you some of this information at no charge. Currently, two good sources are <www.alexa.com> and <www.hoover.com>. They can give you information concerning traffic — ranking the number of visitors in comparison to other sites on the Internet. They can tell you who links to a particular site, and even who visits or uses the site. You're identifying your potential market.

Once you have your own Web site, you can get data via your own applications by installing the following:

- *Comment Pages:* These pages give your visitors a chance to tell you about your Web site, products, and customer service.
- *Chatrooms:* This area of your site gives you a chance to review conversations between individuals as they talk about your industry, your product and/or service.
- *Surveys:* These can give you immediate feedback on specific questions relating to your business.
- *Mailing List:* This can give you direct communication with your customers. The numbers of subscribers should continue to grow. By keeping track of the sign-ups you can compare these figures to the number of visitors who come to your site on a daily basis.

All this can help you with your market research.

How can you use those figures? If you run a "special" on a sale item, and your average number of visitors doesn't change, but you have a dramatic growth in mailing list sign-ups, this tells you that your special sparked an interest ... even if sales on the special item didn't sell exceptionally well.

VAPORWARE

Vaporware is a term for software that was never made. The term first appeared at tradeshows with sales people trying to play catch-up. "Oh, yes, we have that same application on our new product ..." Some people offer products for sale that just plain don't exist — Vaporware.

Firms will list a product on their Web site they would like to sell. If they receive a whole bunch of orders, they complete manufacturing of the product and fill the orders. If they receive no orders or a very limited number of orders, they simply cancel the orders and explain, "Due to manufacturer delays the product has been withdrawn from the market." It's a very crass way of doing business, but it is a very effective use of market research — get orders, make the product or, no orders, no product.

If you have a product, that's a good start. You can use focus groups to help you develop a great name — catchy, easy to remember — but on the Internet you are better off having an address (nothing says you have to have only one URL or Web address) that contains one or more of the keywords for your product. Until you are really well-known, people on the Internet will probably find you from general searches rather than focused searches looking for you directly. For example, let's say you are located in Edmonton and you want to establish a silver finishing company and you primarily want to work for clients in that area. You want the name QuikSilver. The first thing you should use the Internet for is to find out if there are any trademarks for QuickSilver or QuikSilver and then check out the URL <www.silver-plating-Edmonton.com.ca>.

GOOD SOFTWARE AND LINKS

There are numerous add-ons for Web sites that can help you collect market research data. Two of the most useful are counters and site search engines.

Counters

Counters tell you how many people visited your Web site. Depending on the counter, they can also tell you more information about your visitors. Some counters will only tell you the number of visitors you have. Other counters will give you the number of visitors and a short list of the last few visitors and their IP address. Each computer carries its own address, or IP, which identifies a visitor.

Here are three resources for free counters:

- <www.bcentral.com/products/fc/default.asp>
- <www.free-hit-counters.com/>
- <www.prtracker.com/FreeCounter.html>

A good free site for information is <http://www.arin.net/whois/arinwhois.html>, where you can check out their searchable IP address database to see who your visitors are. You merely enter the IP address and see where your visitor comes from. If the visitor is from a large company, the database will reveal that. If your visitor is searching the Internet from their own computer, then the database will just give you general browser information (i.e., Internet Explorer, Netscape).

What's the difference between a free service and a paid service? Sometimes very little. Generally, a free service is only free because they place an advertisement or banner on your site. Stability is usually the problem. Sites that offer free services often disappear. This means that you or someone you hire has to go through your Web site and eliminate dead (nonworking) links and establish new ones. Paid sites also disappear, so paying for a service doesn't mean that it will always be there, but if you don't want the extra advertising on your site, it's better to pay for the service.

Most free sites offer upgrades. These upgrades can give you more services and remove advertising from your site. You will have to weigh the risks and advantages of service against your needs in choosing between a free service, a free service with upgrades, or a software purchase.

You can search for other software to help you track your customers. For example, a product called WebTracker not only allows you to count visitors to your page but it also tells you what browser they are using, the operating system they are running, and if they are visitors returning to your site. You can even find out what time of day most people are visiting your site. More information about WebTracker can be found at <www.fxweb.com/tracker/>.

Site search engines

Site search engines allow visitors to find information on your Web site. If you have a Web site featuring only a few pages, then this isn't anything to worry about. But if you have an extensive Web site, a site search engine helps visitors navigate your site.

A site search engine we recommend is Sitelevel <http://sitelevel.whatuseek.com/>. They have a free service, but we pay to have their advertising removed. Actually, we wouldn't mind if it was their own advertising, but the advertising they use on their pages sometimes comes from our competition, and it's never a good idea to advertise your competition on your own Web site.

Sitelevel offers the following:

- Statistics updated hourly. You can go back 60 days for information.
- Search Counter
- Top Search Queries
- Queries with No Results
- Top Clicked Search Results
- Search Box Results (most popular pages for searches)
- Visitor Statistics (by platform)

Site search engines like Sitelevel *spider* your site. This means their software searches through each page of information. Some search engines do this on a regular basis, which keeps the search information up-to-date. Although the site search engine runs from another Web site (off-site), you still control what it finds. You can select the pages that it will search through. This way you can have pages that are not accessible to everyone.

Charting

We chart the progress of sales and visitors. This is extremely easy when using statistical information supplied by Web programs like counters and affiliate sales reports. We simply use graph paper. You can do the same or you could use Excel or almost any other database program. There are also sophisticated statistical programs you can purchase and use. The choice is yours depending upon your budget and preferences.

By charting your progress, either of Internet related information or non-Internet related information, it may be possible to see changes as they occur. By looking over past histories, you may be able to predict your business more accurately. If you maintain monthly sales data for several years, you may be able to see down periods. For example, if you see that sales lag dramatically in March and April, you may want to schedule your vacation during that time. Or if you have others working for you, then you may want to plan more advertising at that time.

If you have charted your advertising, you may be able to compare advertising to sales. Do sales come immediately upon advertising? Do sales come soon after? Months after? How does your advertising work for sales? If in comparison to the above example of a March-April decline you know that advertising results in sales one month after you advertised, then you know that to boost sales in March and April you should advertise in February and March.

The owner of a direct mail company confided in us that sales were remarkably down in July, but he knew they were always down in July. This July seemed like the worst one ever. He went to his charts — statistically, it was the best July ever! That should have been good news, but his company's revenues were still down from the previous months. It was nice to know, however, that even the worst month still showed an increase in sales.

You can also use charting in other ways. You can make your Web site easier to use, and you can also improve sales with charting. By checking a site search engine, you can chart the keywords to see what people are looking for. If people are looking for information that should be easily found on your site, then perhaps your current navigation headings are too hard to read. You could re-do your navigation headings and then chart the results. If the number of searches for that particular information go down dramatically, you can be fairly certain that you have improved your Web site.

Searches on your site search engine might reveal a needed feature for your product or even a product line. If you have a brown widget and there are numerous searches for pink widgets, then you might want to consider offering a pink widget for sale in addition to your brown one.

The Internet and market research form a marriage made in heaven. Market research runs on data or information, and the Internet is run by data and information. Using basic techniques, you can gather information on your product and your competition. You can conduct surveys and look for surveys from others. You can ask for information directly from your visitors, and in addition, you can find out even more information from them through software applications without intruding on them personally.

From Personal Experience: Don Doman

I have a fairly new business. It's an e-commerce site that sells business and employee training products: <www.ideasandtraining.com>. Many of my products are high-end, big-ticket items. I use Amazon to help balance out price ranges by adding lower-priced items and to present a wider variety of products for sale than I could ever stock or list. The Amazon affiliate program is a market research treasure.

Amazon offers a great selection of statistical information. They have headings for traffic (visitors) and earnings. Here is a list of their reports:

Amazon Earnings Reports

- Earnings by item
- Earnings by quarter
- Earnings by specified time period

Traffic Reports

- Traffic summary with unique visitors, clicks, items ordered on Amazon, items ordered in the Marketplace (additional Amazon 3rd Party Sites)
- Daily traffic — any given day
- Traffic by items (orders)
- Traffic by click-through (A click-through — sometimes called a click-thru — results when someone sees a link on a page, clicks on the link, and is "clicked-thru" to another page or site.)
- Traffic by linking method
- Total traffic
- Traffic by quarter
- Traffic by specified time period

I began my business in June 2001, but use April 2002 as my baseline for my training-site business. That's when it started taking the shape I wanted. I initially used Amazon's affiliate program with either a search box or keyword links. Amazon pays out when you reach a minimum of $25 in sales. I had never received a payment from Amazon, so you can see I was starting at ground zero.

At the end of March, I noted that I had some sales on Amazon. In business, sales equal encouragement.

Armed with my list of books that had sold in the first quarter, I developed a page of "Best Sellers." Of course, any book that actually sold on Amazon from my site became an instant best seller for me. My list of best sellers was market research data. I earned a 5 percent commission on those titles. I had several books that sold multiple copies — real best sellers. My next step was to use direct links for those titles. Direct links to Amazon books pays a 15 percent commission instead of the lowly 5 percent of regular sales (from a generic link).

I set a goal for my Amazon book sales: $1 a day. That sounds extremely low, but it's more than many people earn on Amazon. A dollar a day pays my Web site hosting charges, and my on-site search engine.

Many affiliate programs offer instant account information. Sometimes Amazon's data lags by nearly a week. This is annoying, but still very workable. Some affiliate programs do not give specific product sales data. Now that is a major irritant.

Account information is data that helps judge how you are doing for both traffic and sales. Sales often lag behind traffic. People see what they want, but come back later to purchase. Amazon gives data for both traffic and earnings. Earnings are limited to shipped items.

This sales (earnings) data is extremely useful. For instance, during April on Amazon for my Ideas and Training site, I noticed that a good-selling book was *The Big Book of Customer Service Games.* I added direct links to that book and found six other Big Book Games selections. I added those seven books to a table at the top of my Business Games and Activities product page.

For April, May, and June, I made 14 regular sales and 5 direct sales for *The Big Book of Customer Service Games.* In addition, I made one direct sale and 13 regular sales of the other Big Book Games products. So, by using market research statistics that told me I had sold a few books of one title in the first quarter of the year, I was able to make 33 sales in the next quarter — an increase of 1000 percent!

In addition to market research information in the form of reports, Amazon also has affiliate discussion boards. You can use these discussion boards to answer questions you have about the program in general and use it to find out particular data and information as well. As with some market research surveys, the data still has to be viewed with a judgmental eye — some people have been known to exaggerate.

On the discussion boards, you'll find questions such as, "Why am I not getting visitors and sales?" Or, you'll find "Why am I not getting very much traffic?" The answers to these questions help you put your own statistics and information in context.

For example, in a recent response to sales, someone wrote that they had their own search engine site and managed to send 4000 visitors a day (that's a lot) to Amazon. The owner of the site had a generic banner on their main page that sent generic visitors to Amazon. Some bought, but many didn't. It was strictly a numbers game. Those numbers are important statistics. Knowing how many visitors you need to send to Amazon to make a sale can be sobering.

The same thing applies to visitors to your own site. It's nice to know how many visitors you need to get to your site to make a sale or referral. You should know that same information holds true whether it means visitors to your brick-and-mortar store or a virtual storefront.

If you make a $10 sale for every 100 visitors to your site and you need to make $500 a day, then statistics tell you that you need to average 5,000 visitors a day. If you have only ten visitors a day, then you'll make a sale approximately every week and a half. These sobering statistics help you evaluate your advertising needs, your budget, and the future of your business.

In the above Amazon associate example, the owner of the search engine site did not make a remarkable amount of sales in terms of a visitor-to-sales ratio when compared to my own site. If I sent Amazon 4000 visitors a day, I'd be jumping up and down. On a good day I send 65 visitors and make a few sales.

Traffic reports for my site tell me many things. My baseline numbers are very revealing. For the second quarter, my average daily number of visitors (from Amazon data) was only 33. That's a long way from 4000! However, my sales were comparable to the guy with a search engine and his 4,000 visitors a day.

April

32 Items Shipped

$539.32 in Total Sales

$34.74 in Commissions

$1.16 per Day

667 Visitors — 22 per Day

May

47 Items Shipped

$1020.46 in Total Sales

$62.73 in Commissions

$2.02 per Day

1063 Visitors — 34 per Day

June

51 Items Shipped

$860.69 in Total Sales

$46.02 in Commissions

$1.53 per Day

1263 Visitors — 42 per Day

What do these figures tell us about my relationship with Amazon? In April I began using the direct-linking method to their products. This took weeks to change, and implementation didn't begin until the second week of April. Sales in May grew by 50 percent, but revenues nearly doubled due to the direct-linking method I began using.

Looking over the Amazon statistics, you might draw the conclusion that even though visitors increased to nearly twice what they were in April, sales decreased in June to almost what they had been in April. What's missing? At the end of June there were 16 sales that had not been shipped. Those sales were reflected in the following month.

This is important to remember. Sometimes you can use statistics immediately and sometimes you need to use statistics over a longer period of time to draw proper conclusions. Always look outside your statistics for missing information.

By the end of August, my total sales for the month were just shy of my total sales for the entire second quarter. Amazon shipped more items for me in August than the complete earlier (second) quarter. At the end of the month there were almost two dozen items that were ordered but not shipped. The number of visitors only increased by a couple of hundred people, but sales increased dramatically. The reports revealed there were several multiple purchases. One sale resulted in 62 copies sold. This book had only one previous sale ... perhaps the purchaser bought the book, read it, and then ordered for the entire staff. I like to think that my customers keep returning.

Viewers come to my site looking for business training. I focus on business and employee training. The products I recommend on Amazon reflect the interest of my visitors. For instance, I would never link the latest Emeril cookbook (although, I did make a sale of it), even though I like his television show and his recipes. What I link to from my site is dependent upon the interests of my visitors. I know what their interests are based on their choices, and that is revealed to me in my market research data: Amazon reports. I use the data to target the needs and wants of my visitors.

I can't list every book that Amazon features, but I can list those in which my visitors are interested. Earnings reports tell me what is selling, and traffic reports tell me what titles generate click-throughs. Using data from those reports helps me weed out what doesn't sell and more prominently feature what does sell.

Chapter 8
PRIMARY DATA: YOUR SURVEY METHODS

CHOOSE THE SURVEY METHOD THAT ACCOMPLISHES YOUR GOAL

There are many methods of market research, from the orthodox to the extraordinary. *Anything* you do that helps you find out who's buying, why they're buying, where they're buying, how much they're spending, how they feel about your company, etc., can be considered market research.

> *Find out how your current customers found you. Then put more of your efforts in that direction.*
>
> CAROL ROBERTS

A radio station that issues bumper stickers reading *Honk if you love station XYZ* is conducting market research if it keeps track of the beeps it hears. A store that holds a sale is conducting market research if it keeps track of the best-selling items and uses the data to help it determine what items to put on sale next time. A museum is conducting market research if it lowers its admission rates for a month and tracks how many more (or fewer) people visit as a result.

We hope you will do everyday market research like this as long as you are in business. You can get as creative as you want in your techniques.

This chapter covers several of the most standard, effective surveying techniques you are most likely to use when —

(a) starting your business,

(b) expanding your business, or

(c) finding the best way to maintain your business in a changing market.

The most common methods of primary research are:

(a) Polls/questionnaires
  - (i) By phone
  - (ii) In person (in the respondent's home, at a shopping mall, at your business, or other locations)
  - (iii) Direct mail
  - (iv) In a magazine, newspaper, or newsletter
  - (v) Table tents and counter cards

(b) Focus groups

(c) Product or service sampling

> *Ex ungue leonem ("from a claw, the lion") — From a sample we can judge the whole.*
>
> LATIN PROVERB

POLLS/QUESTIONNAIRES

Whether you test your product or service, ask people to evaluate your advertising, or merely ask people about their likes, dislikes, habits, and purchasing plans, you will often be using questionnaires to collect the data you need.

But how and where should you administer your questionnaire? How long should it be? What are the advantages and disadvantages of different polling methods? Are certain times better than others? How do you know who to interview, and how do you screen them? Table 2 shows the various methods of polling and how they compare.

You can also gather data via an online survey if you have a Web site. Results are generally reliable but often suffer from limited responses since your audience itself may be rather small.

HOW TO SELECT AND SCREEN YOUR INTERVIEW SUBJECTS

The accuracy of your data depends in part on the size and makeup of your survey group. In general, the larger the group, the less chance of error.

Number in Sample	Chance of Error
100	10%
300	6%
500	5%
1,000	3%

Your group must also reflect, as accurately as possible, the makeup of your target audience. You must be careful not to unconsciously make choices which bias your survey results. For example, if your target audience contains people of various races or ethnic groups, you must be careful to include a representative number of these people in your survey. If you believe your potential target customers live throughout the city, you must be careful not to do your surveying in only one neighborhood.

Just as you must make sure to *include* a representative sampling of members of your target audience, you must be sure to *exclude* those who are not in your target, or to limit the numbers of people who want to participate if your sample is already large or representative enough. If you do your surveying at a shopping mall, for example, you may find teenagers eager to participate. That's fine if they're your target; otherwise you must find a polite, efficient way of screening them out.

Your interviewers should be armed with two or three questions designed to do this job. For instance, if you are conducting a phone survey intended only for homemakers, your interviewer might begin your call asking for the woman of the house. The first question to her (after a brief introduction) might be, "Do you earn an income outside the home?" If she says yes, she does not qualify. The interviewer might then ask if anyone else in the house could be described as a full-time homemaker. If not, the interviewer would courteously conclude the interview.

If you employ several interviewers working simultaneously, you have an additional difficulty. Each interviewer may be getting a fairly representative selection, but you must periodically "check in" during the survey period to make sure that overall the sample remains representative of your target group.

Some survey methods, like direct mail, allow you little opportunity to do screening once the questionnaire is in the recipient's hands. However, you can pre-screen by choosing the right mailing list to reach your target. This is where your customer lists come in so handy.

Figures don't always mean what they seem to say. In a recent Gallup survey publicized all over Canada, 56 percent of respondents said they thought Canadian men had unfair advantages over women. The media called this a significant increase from a recent year, when only 53 percent held that opinion. However, buried at the bottom of the news stories was the information that the poll had a 3.1 percent margin of error. In other words, the difference between 53 percent and 56 percent was insignificant — a statistical glitch.

Robert Fulford

Globe and Mail, March 24, 1993

USING MAILING LISTS

When you plan to conduct a survey by mail, you will need a list containing names and addresses of a good, representative sample of your target audience. If you already have a customer/prospect list that fills your need, great. If not, you will probably need to rent a mailing list.

TABLE 2
POLLS AND QUESTIONNAIRES

METHOD	MAXIMUM TIME	BEST TIME
By phone	15 minutes	For people at home: evening hours after dinner. For people at work: office hours; not Monday morning or Friday afternoon.
In person — in the respondent's home	Up to an hour	Evening hours after dinner; Saturdays; by appointment
In person — at a shopping mall	5 to 15 minutes	Daytime hours; evenings after dinner; Sundays
In person — at your business[1]	Depends on nature of business	Whenever customers or clients are least hurried
In person — other locations (clubs, schools, senior centers, etc.)	Varies	Whenever people are unhurried, relaxed, and not under any type of pressure or influence from you.
Direct mail	5 to 15 minutes	Not applicable, but try not to have your mailing arrive on a Monday, or at the subject's home on a Wednesday. These are the days on which your survey is most likely to be thrown away.
In a magazine, newspaper, or newsletter	Varies	Varies; often weekend edition of newspaper is best
Table tents and counter cards	Very brief; 2 to 3 minutes	Leave them out all the time
Online	Varies	Leave them on all the time

1. Since every business is different, you will need to judge many of these factors for yourself. For example, if your business is one in which customers sit in a waiting room prior to or during your service, you have an excellent opportunity to interview them or have them fill out a survey form. If your business is retail, on the other hand, you have only moments in which to stop and survey them.

TABLE 2 — Continued

ADVANTAGES	DISADVANTAGES
Fast; no large staff required; good response rate; ability to control sample size and makeup; can ask complex questions and probe for detail; interviewer isn't as likely to influence the subject; can monitor the interviewers to make sure they are doing their job well	Consumers are increasingly fed up with telemarketing and surveying; can't show product, packaging, etc.
Ability to show product or service; can ask the largest number of questions per respondent; can ask complex questions and probe for maximum detail; good ability to control sample makeup; relaxed, atmosphere; good response rate	Highest cost per interview; large staff required; much time required; difficult to find people at home, except by appointment; strong possibility interviewer will personally influence subject
Ability to show product or service; ability to visually identify some demographic characteristics; can ask relatively complex questions and probe for some detail; good response rate	High cost; interrupting people who may be busy; difficult to control makeup of sample; inability to ask complex, probing questions; difficult to monitor interviewers; possibility that interviewer will influence subject
Ability to show product or service; good ability to control makeup of sample; can ask relatively complex questions and probe for detail; good-to-adequate response rate; relatively low cost per interview	Interrupting people who may be busy; possibility that interviewer will influence subject
Can conduct lengthy, detailed surveys, similar to in-home surveys, but at less expense and in more controlled conditions.	Similar to above
Very wide sample distribution possible (national or worldwide); can show photos of product; no interviewer influence; about same cost-per-interview as phone research; people can respond when they are not hurried or pressured	Slow; can take weeks or months to get all responses; no complex questions or explanations possible; mailing lists may be outdated; impossible to control sample makeup; you don't know who's actually responding and you have no way of verifying any statements; respondents are most likely to be those with vested interests
Same as direct mail except for variation in sample distribution based on circulation of publication	No complex questions or explanations possible; impossible to control sample makeup; you don't know who's actually responding; respondents are most likely to be those with vested interests
Inexpensive; can show product; easy for people to respond; no interviewer influence	No complex questions or explanations possible; difficult to control sample makeup; in a small business, people may be unconsciously influenced by you or your employees
Always up-to-date	May have limited responses

There are literally thousands of mailing lists available, covering interests and occupations from animal rights activists to xylophone players. You can rent lists of business executives, engineers, computer users, housewives, musicians, horse owners, Corvette lovers, stamp collectors — you name it.

Better yet, the larger lists are usually available in various breakdowns, allowing you to target even more specifically. For example, you might be able to rent a list of Arabian-horse owners with incomes over $100,000 living in Northern California, or a list of male outdoor enthusiasts who own a certain brand of fishing tackle. The list you need is probably out there. But how do you find and rent it?

Beginning your search

If you don't already know of a possible list, hit a medium or larger library and look in the reference section for copies of *Standard Rate and Data Service* (SRDS) (in the United States) or *Canadian Advertising Rates and Data* (CARD) (in Canada). You will find entire issues of these phone-book-sized directories dedicated to mailing lists.

Check the alphabetical listing section for the lists you need (auctioneers, *Time* magazine subscribers, mothers, florists, Lillian Vernon catalogue customers, etc.), then start calling. In most cases, the number you call will belong to a list broker (a person who rents other people's lists) or a list compiler (a company that assembles lists of its own from other sources).

The compiler or broker can tell you how many people are on each list (for instance, 12,700 sand and gravel dealers, 6,685 hospital gift shops, or 125,900 farmers with 1,000 acres or more), what breakdowns are available, and how much the list costs. Now the negotiation begins.

Types of lists

Though you may not see it spelled out in SRDS or CARD, there are basically two types of lists available, and the differences are important. If you can't tell what kind of list you've found in a directory, ask the broker. The two are —

(a) compiled lists, and

(b) responder lists.

Compiled lists

Compiled lists are, as the name implies, lists of names, addresses (and, sometimes, phone numbers) taken from other sources. Typically they come from phone books, club membership rosters, professional association membership lists, government licensing lists, and various types of directories. They also include people who have purchased certain types of products or made certain investments. Typical examples: people who live within postal code V7J 1H1 or zip code 95008, purchasers of large boats, and members of country clubs.

Compiled lists are easy to rent. You just call the list owner or broker and, once your credit is established, place an order by phone. The list comes in a week or two, in the form of ready-to-use labels that you can apply by hand or machine.

Compiled lists are also cheap. A typical charge is $45 to $65 per thousand names.

But compiled lists have two major, inherent weaknesses. First, because they are made up of names of individuals who may or may not ever have responded to mail solicitations, they contain a high percentage of people who will simply pitch your survey in the wastebasket without even looking at it. On average, 30 percent of the recipients from a compiled list will do exactly that.

The second great drawback is that these lists are often woefully out of date. Though list compilers usually claim to "clean" their lists quarterly, this is not always so. As many as 50 percent of the names on a list that hasn't been updated in two years may be obsolete.

Responder lists

Responder lists are, as their name implies, made up of people whose names, addresses, and/or phone numbers got on the list because they responded to a mail solicitation. These typically include magazine subscribers, catalogue or mail-order buyers, and members of national special-interest organizations which solicit by mail, like The Nature Conservancy or the National Rifle Association.

Responder lists are harder to rent. In each case, the names on these lists represent some company's valued customers or some organization's cherished contributors. The list owners are not about to rent their names to anyone who might —

(a) compete with the owner,

(b) harass the people on the list, or

(c) send mailings that might insult or offend the recipients.

If you want to rent a responder list, be prepared to send a copy of your survey or other mailing, then wait weeks until the list owner gives his or her approval. Be prepared to be turned down for reasons you may not even understand.

Responder lists are also expensive. They often cost 25¢ or 35¢ *per name* ($250 to $350 per thousand names), and may cost $1 or more per name. But you are usually getting a much higher quality list. You already know that 100 percent of these people are willing to respond to mail solicitations of one kind or another. Like compiled lists, they usually come in the form of ready-to-apply labels. If you need the names in some other form, just ask.

Responder lists don't contain the 30 percent waste factor of compiled lists, and they are "cleaned" regularly by the owners.

About reusing rented lists

Lists are rented for one-time use — and the owners mean it. Many direct mailers are tempted to copy the sheets of labels and reuse the names for later mailings. Don't do it. Nearly every mailing list comes with one or more dummy names planted in it. When you send your first and only authorized mailing using the list, a mailing list professional receives a copy of your mailing at the address listed for the "dummy." If you later send an unauthorized mailing to that name, you're in trouble. You may have to pay, and you will never be able to rent from that company again.

There is only one way you can do a second mailing to any of the names on a rented list: if the people respond to your first mailing. Anyone who responds becomes legitimately your prospect or your customer, and you may enter that person's name and address in your database and use it as often as you like.

> Alvin B. Zeller Inc., a provider of mailing lists, surveyed 855 customers, then printed some of the survey results on the inside cover of its mailing list catalogue. Zeller listed the percentages of respondents who referred to Zeller's lists as "excellent" and "superior," and the percentage of those who said they would "definitely buy" again. The survey not only gave Zeller market research data, but a valuable marketing tool.

Response rates

What percentage of the people who receive your survey will respond to it? We wish there were a simple answer to that question. But in fact, responses vary so greatly that no one would predict a response rate without knowing more specific information about your particular mailing.

In general, response rates depend on three major factors:

(a) The quality of the list

(b) How targeted your mailing is to recipients' interests

(c) The quality of your mailing

By quality of your mailing we don't mean how fancy or slick it is. We mean how carefully crafted it is to appeal to the interests of those who receive it.

There are some other factors that can increase response:

(a) Offer a time limit and/or an incentive (like a discount certificate on your services)

(b) Use first-class postage when you send the mailing

(c) Pay the return postage

For a very untargeted mailing to a compiled list, you may get a response of 1 percent or less. For a very targeted mailing to a responder list, you could get 20 percent or more.

You might receive a high percentage response if yours is a small, local business and your mailing goes to customers or prospects who are predisposed to like you. You may also get a high rate of response if people are angry with you and want to let off steam. So remember, your goal is not always to get the largest response, but to get the most balanced, representative response from the highest quality list you can afford.

USING FOCUS GROUPS

Most questionnaires yield results that can be categorized and statistically analyzed. This is quantitative data. Focus groups produce qualitative data — data that can't be expressed in numbers. They help you determine how your target customer thinks and feels, and how he or she might react to your marketing plans.

> *We are all of us, more or less, the slaves of opinion.*
>
> WILLIAM HAZLITT

A focus group is basically nothing more than a few people gathered around a table to discuss a particular subject. Members of the group are carefully chosen, usually to fit the description of your best target customer.

Focus groups can be used to learn a variety of things. A focus group could review your packaging, advertising, service, or even the taste of your product. You could call a group together when planning to expand your business, change your corporate image, add a new service, or change your market positioning.

Nickelodeon, the cable television network for children, is probably the largest user of focus groups in the children's market. Once they come up with a format for a new show, they hire a producer to tape a pilot. Then they ask focus groups to review the proposed program. In 1990, they conducted between 200 and 250 focus groups, using the children's input to help design new programs. In 1991, their revenues increased to $167.5 million, up 21 percent.

Advertising Age,
February 10, 1992

What can a focus group do that a questionnaire can't? Here's an example. A company planning to market a new sauce asks members of its target audience to come together to sample the product, examine the proposed packaging, and respond to proposed ads. In this case, the focus group can do what individual taste tests or tests of packaging could not do: give the marketer an idea of how his or her entire marketing presentation works together. The company might learn that people perceived the taste as being too sophisticated for the packaging, or that the advertising doesn't emphasize the most important benefit of the product. Only a focus group can give you this kind of "fuzzy" information.

A focus group is different than a brainstorming session in that it is made up exclusively of members of your target market and is designed to discover their feelings and perceptions rather than to elicit their ideas.

Members of focus groups are usually paid, but you may be able to call friends and customers together for free. Just be aware that even the best focus groups don't produce scientific data. Members are subject to being influenced by each other, by the group leader, or by what they think you want to hear. A group of friends may be especially reluctant to tell the whole truth and nothing but the truth if it means giving you bad news.

To make your focus group as effective as possible, consider the following tips:

(a) Choose a group of six to ten people who represent your target market.

(b) Set up an audio or video recorder, preferably where it will not be distracting. Use more than one microphone, if necessary, to adequately capture everyone's comments.

(c) Make everyone comfortable and welcome; let them know their ideas are important.

(d) Clearly explain what you would like them to discuss; have a loose outline of topics or questions prepared.

(e) Have each person describe his or her experience with the product or service, then open the gathering for group discussion.

(f) Allow for creative conversation, but make sure the talk doesn't wander off on unrelated topics for too long.

(g) Don't let the easy talkers dominate — draw everyone out.

(h) Summarize periodically and ask the group to confirm that your summary is correct.

(i) Afterward, analyze the results.

PRODUCT OR SERVICE SAMPLING

Will your product taste good? Be in good taste? Be acceptable? Be something people can't do without? Will it be easy to understand and use? Will your service have unexpected glitches? Some questions you'll never be able to answer until you have people actually try your product or service.

Many times, you will need samples of your product or service to accompany your surveys or focus groups. If your product is inexpensive to make, you should do a limited production run for the test.

If you are testing a complex, manufactured product, you should have a prototype made. The prototype should be a full-scale working model that people can handle, take apart, operate — whatever they are supposed to do with the real thing. Having a prototype manufactured can be expensive, but the prototype does double duty; it helps your market research and helps you work out problems in the product itself.

If you are testing a service, you probably don't need to produce anything, unless your service requires the support of specialized tools, custom software, literature, etc. Produce what you need and no more.

Sampling tips

If you are testing an item of food or drink, or any other item that lends itself to comparison, you may want to test a sample of your product versus a sample of a competitor's product. In other cases, you can conduct what's called a single-sample test using your product by itself and getting people's reactions.

When doing comparison tests, you should not show the name of either product. People are influenced by name brands, and may automatically rate a better-known product more favorably.

For the same reason, you should never show the packaging or advertising of a product unless that's part of what you're testing. Avoid anything that might unduly influence people.

When doing comparisons with food products, keep switching the order in which you give the samples. In taste tests, people are biased toward the first sample.

> Victoria Cunningham, owner of The Right Angle Advertising Services of Washington, offered this suggestion to a Cajun-cooking specialties developer. Allow people to sample your product, and if they like it, ask them to send a postcard to their supermarkets urging them to carry your products. If this inexpensive, backdoor sales technique generates 50 to 100 requests, no supermarket will say no.
>
> *Inc.*, February, 1992

Approach Software of California used a direct-mail campaign to test market their new database application. They sent similar mailings to three different groups, offering one group an introductory price of $99, another a price of $129, and the third group a price of $149. Sales were comparable for the $129 and $149 mailings, so Approach settled on $149 as it's "official" introductory price when it introduced the product to the mass market.

Inc., February, 1993

Test marketing

What we've been talking about above is product or service sampling, the purpose of which is to get comments about the item you're about to market.

There's also *test marketing*, a different but related technique in which you take your product (which has presumably already been tested by a targeted sample group) and offer it for sale on a limited or experimental basis. You can place it in different types of stores, in different geographic locations, in different packaging, at different prices, using different advertising, etc., to determine what approach works best.

Case Study

Clarice Rogers decides to hold an informal focus group, showing her existing prototype address book to a small group selected from her target audience. Many of the people she chooses are her friends, while others are acquaintances from her business life: a stockbroker, her attorney, and a woman who runs a large regional craft fair.

The goals of the focus group are —

(a) to verify that her target audience has an interest in the product,

(b) to get their opinions on how to improve the book,

(c) to get a feel for what women would be willing to pay for it, and

(d) to learn what she can about what medium is most likely to reach her target.

The group produces some encouraging news and a few surprises. The best news: her target will buy the book — if she gets their attention with some great advertising or packaging.

One participant suggests she improve the book by making it loose-leaf; buyers would purchase the expensive binding only once, then buy new inserts each year. Clarice is thrilled with the idea. It not only makes the book more affordable in the long run, but it gives Clarice the opportunity to establish a continuing relationship with her buyers.

The group also produces a list of potential media to explore, from the *Wall Street Journal* to the local *Scene* magazine. The women also name a number of catalogues and direct marketing companies from which they regularly buy.

The one area in which the group doesn't help her is price. As before, when that subject comes up, the answers are all over the board, from $15 to $75. She decides she will poll customers at a nearby upscale mall, again showing them her book. Her polling will share many of the same goals as her focus group, but will yield more quantifiable data.

Finally, she plans to make up additional prototype books and place them with three carefully chosen executive women. After the women have used the books for a month, she will sit down with each of them and spend an hour asking detailed questions about how they used the book and how she could improve it. Again, she will focus on questions of price. She knows her book will necessarily be much higher priced than the average appointment book, and that she must choose carefully if she is to find a price to fit the luxury image of the product without turning customers off.

Chapter 9 WRITING A QUESTIONNAIRE

THREE ELEMENTS OF A SUCCESSFUL QUESTIONNAIRE

> *Online surveys only produce a fraction of responses compared to quizzes.*
>
> HAL SLATER, AUTHOR OF *HIGH TICKET SELLING*

You want your questionnaire to be as effective as possible — one that people will be willing to respond to, and one which will yield accurate, useful information to help make your venture successful.

When composing your questionnaire, there are several important things you must always do:

(a) Make it the right length

(b) Make sure the questions are clear and unambiguous

(c) Make sure the questions aren't leading

Make it the right length

As you saw in the last chapter, the length of your questionnaire is governed largely by the place you administer it and the method by which you administer it.

A survey taken at the counter of a retail store should rarely exceed five or six questions, while a survey conducted by an interviewer in a person's home could easily have one hundred or more questions.

You are unlikely to be able to learn everything you want to know in one survey, anyway, so one way to control the length of your questionnaire is to begin by writing all the questions you'd like to ask, then begin eliminating them, question by question, until you've reached a compromise: the maximum number of questions you can ask in the maximum amount of time your chosen method will allow.

Before administering the questionnaire to your survey group, test it on a couple of members of your target audience. Administer it to them exactly as it is meant to be done during the survey, by phone or in person, self-administered or with an interviewer. This will help you gauge the time it takes and will also help you clear up any hard-to-understand or misleading questions.

People on the Internet seem to be in a hurry. They want information and they want it now! Surveys take time, so you may need high amounts of traffic before you receive an adequate number of replies for a good sampling.

However, the same people who bypass an onsite survey often jump at the chance to test their knowledge with a quiz. If you can change your survey questions into a quiz format, you can generally boost your responses. With a quiz you have a chance to entertain and educate your visitors while you gather data and add new e-mail addresses to your mailing list (as a common practice you should ask for e-mail addresses, just like you should ask for business cards at a networking meeting).

Make sure the questions are clear and unambiguous

Take a look at this question from a beverage marketer's survey:

- What beverages do you drink?
  - ❑ Coffee
  - ❑ Tea
  - ❑ Cola
  - ❑ Non-cola soft drink
  - ❑ Fruit juice
  - ❑ Milk
  - ❑ Other (explain)____________________

This question is inadequate for several reasons. First, it doesn't make it clear whether the respondent may check a number of boxes, or whether he or she is supposed to select only one. Since the question says *beverages*, plural, you may think it's obvious, but it isn't. When confronted with multiple choices, a lot of people automatically assume they're only allowed one. You must be explicit about instructions.

Will anyone plunk down actual money for what you're planning to offer? I knew I didn't want to start a company where I had to beg for business.

PHILLIP CROSBY

Second, the question is too broad. Confronted with this question, most of us would be justified checking off every box. After all, haven't most of us, at some time or another, drunk most of the listed drinks?

Here are a few ways the question could have been improved:

- Which beverage or beverages do you drink in an average day? (Check all that apply)
- Which beverages do you drink regularly? (Check all that apply)
- Which beverage do you drink most frequently? (Check only one)

Time to consult a pro? A professional market researcher can review your questionnaire to make sure it will yield the most clear and useful data. Consider spending a few hundred dollars to get expert advice here. For a little more, the researcher could design your questionnaire for you.

In general:

(a) Keep questions short and easy to understand.

(b) Ask for only one piece of information in each question.

(c) Keep the target audience in mind (how educated are they, how familiar with your product or service, etc.).

(d) Always double check to make sure the meaning of the question is clear.

(e) Give enough instructions to tell the respondent exactly how to respond.

Make sure the questions aren't leading

It's very important to ask questions in such a way that you get the respondent's true views, not the answer you want to hear. There are many factors that can influence the person taking the survey: for example, the interviewer's attitude or tone, the setting, and so on. Do your best to control them all. The best place to start is with your questions.

These are typical leading questions:

- Did you like our convenient layaway policy? ____________
- Many people have told us they like our selection of merchandise. Do you agree?
- Do you believe our competitor is too high priced?

Here's how to make those questions less leading:

- Did our layaway policy meet your needs?
- Was our selection of merchandise (circle one)

  Excellent Very good Good Fair Poor
- How did our prices compare to those of similar businesses (circle one)?

  Lower Same Higher

FOUR TYPES OF QUESTIONS

Judge a man by his questions rather than by his answers.

Voltaire

Generally there are four types of questions you can use in a survey:

(a) Two-choice

(b) Multiple-choice

(c) Ranking

(d) Open-ended

Two-choice

Two-choice questions give the respondent an either/or selection:

- Do you drink coffee? ❑ Yes ❑ No
- Do you prefer this item in ❑ Black ❑ Gray (Please check one)
- Would you recommend our service to your friends? ❑ Yes ❑ No

Multiple-choice

Multiple-choice questions allow the respondent to choose one or more possibilities from a list:

- What community service organizations do you belong to: (Check all that apply)

___ Jaycees
___ Rotary
___ Lions
___ Optimists
___ Kiwanis
___ Sertoma
___ Other (list)________________________________

When using multiple choice, it's important to include as many options as you can, certainly not leaving out any major ones. Before writing the above question, for instance, the marketer determined the names of all the service organizations in town. If the questionnaire had neglected to list Kiwanis, for example, many Kiwanis members might not have added it to the "Other" category, and the results would be unbalanced.

It's a sure bet that some respondents will also check the "Other" category and list organizations such as Mensa or their softball league which don't fit the category of community service organizations. In that case, however, no harm has been done; those responses can be discarded without affecting the value of the survey. Or you might even be able to use these entries as miscellaneous data.

Ranking

There are several forms of ranking questions. The most common one gives respondents a scale on which to evaluate a single item:

- How would you rate the flavor of our chicken sandwich? (Circle one)

  Excellent   Very Good   Good   Fair   Poor

or

- How would you rate the service you received from your waiter? (Please circle one)

  Poor   Good   Excellent

  1 2 3 4 5 6 7 8 9 10

Other questions ask people to rank a series of items or qualities against other items or qualities:

- What is most important to you? Please place a 1 beside the most important, a 2 beside the second most important, and a 3 beside the third most important.

___ Taste

___ Speed of service

___ Price

or

- Which of our menu items do you purchase most often? Please place a 1 beside the one you most often purchase, a 2 beside your next choice, and so on. If you never purchase an item, put a 0 beside it.

___ Hamburger

___ Chicken sandwich

___ Fish sandwich

___ Fried chicken

___ Taco

___ Burrito

___ Nachos

You could use this type of ranking question, for instance, to ask respondents to rate your company or product against a competing company or product.

For an eye-opening survey, try asking past customers why they no longer buy from you. Ask questions that help you discern why they are no longer your customers and what you can do to bring old customers back or better maintain current customers. The US federal government conducted a survey to find out why people ceased doing business with services. The number one reason: indifference. The number two reason: dissatisfaction with the quality of service. If you have lost customers for either of those reasons, you might win them back simply by surveying them, thus showing you care.

Open-ended

Open-ended questions are used when you need more information than you can get from the other three question types. Open-ended questions are generally used to get qualitative data, while the other three types generally yield quantitative data (because even when they deal with qualities, like taste or convenience, they yield responses you can tally or plot on a chart).

Open-ended questions are often used to elicit detail about a previous two-choice, multiple-choice, or ranking question. For example, after the question asking respondents about the community organizations they belong to, a questionnaire might ask:

- What do you appreciate most about this organization?

or

- What prompted you to join this organization?

While you may find that many people do not respond to open-ended questions, you will find that others appreciate the opportunity to elaborate, and actually develop more positive feelings about your company merely because you give them the opportunity to have their say.

How many types of questions should you use?

Any survey longer than five or six questions will probably use several types of questions. Often, a response to one question will automatically lead to another type of question. For example:

Two-choice:

1. Do you drink cola beverages? Yes No
   (If no, skip to question 4)

Multiple-choice:

2. Which cola is your favorite?
   (Please check only one)

❑ Coca-Cola

❑ Pepsi

❑ RC

❑ Other ______________

Open-ended:

3. Why do prefer this brand?

There is no rule about how, when, or whether to mix question types, but in general a balanced, informative survey will include several types of questions.

OTHER INFORMATION TO INCLUDE ON YOUR QUESTIONNAIRE

Questions aren't the only thing that belong on your questionnaire. You also need:

(a) An introduction

(b) Keying

An introduction

Start your questionnaire with a brief written introduction stating the purpose of your survey. This is absolutely crucial if your survey is not being administered in person. You must have a written introduction on any survey sent via direct mail, published in a newspaper or other publication, or placed on a table or counter for customers to fill out. You should have a written introduction even on surveys administered in person; it will help your interviewer remember to give vital information.

You probably don't need more than a few sentences, which might read something like this:

> I am developing a product for new mothers and am contacting women in Iowa who have recently had babies. Would you please take a moment to tell me how you feel about the following baby supplies?

Notice that the introduction is specific about who is being surveyed; this gives the recipient a sense of belonging to a group. Notice, too, that it is not specific at all about the type of product being developed. This is to avoid having the recipient prejudge the product or the survey. Sample 6 shows how Clarice introduced her survey.

Keying

If your survey is being given in more than one location, administered at several different times, or sent to more than one mailing list, you should always put key letters or numbers on the survey form indicating which location, time, or list the survey is from. Keying is very easy and there's no reason not to do it. Simply print or hand write (whichever is more appropriate) a combination of letters and/or numbers at the top or bottom of the form.

Your key might look something like this:

Key:	Meaning:
DM/1094	Davenport Mall, October, 1994 (an in-person survey)
DF	Dog Fancy magazine mailing list (a direct-mail survey)
CL	My own customer list (a direct-mail survey)
NT/3394	News Tribune March 3, 1994 (a newspaper survey)
3394/7pm	March 3, 1994, 7:00 p.m. (a phone survey)

Why keep track of such minutiae as dates and times? It isn't always necessary, but with an in-person survey or phone survey you may discover that responses are more positive or negative at certain times. If you are using several interviewers in different locations or at different times, keying can also tell you who administered which survey, and can help you track and correct errors one interviewer may be making. (In some cases, you may want to add "Administered by ______________" to help you track each interviewer's work.)

Also, be sure to write down your master keys on another sheet of paper. There's nothing more frustrating than keying all those forms only to find you can't remember later what the keys indicate.

Case Study

Clarice Rogers composed two questionnaires, one for her mall survey, and a longer one to be administered to the three women who will spend a month using her prototype books. Sample 6 shows the shorter of the two. Keep in mind that it is designed to be administered in person with the prototype address book available for the respondents' inspection.

Clarice used a combination of two-choice, multiple-choice, and open-ended questions to elicit different information.

SAMPLE 6
MALL SURVEY

I am developing a product that I believe will be useful to executive women and women with busy social scedules. I would appreciate you taking a few minutes to tell me about your experience with similar products and to help me improve my product.

Part I — Your current product use

1. Do you currently own an appointment book or executive dayminder book?

❑ Yes ❑ No

(If No, please go to Question 6)

2. Do you use your book primarliy for:

❑ Business ❑ Social events ❑ Don't use it

3. How did you acquire your book?

❑ Purchased for myself (Got to Question 4)
❑ Received as gift (Go to Question 5)
❑ Other (Go to Question 6)

4. If you purchased it for yourself, where did you purchase it?

❑ Department store ❑ Specialty store ❑ Catalog
❑ Direct mail ❑ Factory outlet/discount store
❑ Other (please specify) ______________________

5. If you received it as a gift, what was the occasion?

❑ Birthday ❑ Christmas ❑ Anniversary ❑ Graduation
❑ Other (please specify) ______________________

6. Do you own any of the following products?
(Check all that apply)

❑ Attaché or briefcase costing <$150 ❑ Leather-covered notebook or binder
❑ Hardbound art books ❑ Art or calligraphy supplies
❑ Executive pen/pencil set ❑ Executive toys
❑ Leather-bound calculator

SAMPLE 6 — Continued

Part II — Your response to this product

Please examine the *Calligraphy Book of Days* and answer the following questions.

7. Would you consider buying this book?

❑ Yes ❑ No

(If No, please skip to Question 10)

8. How much would you be willing to pay for the *Calligraphy Book of Days*?

____

9. Would you buy this book:

❑ For yourself ❑ As a gift for a woman ❑ As a gift for a man

❑ Other (please specify) ____________________________________

10. What do you find most appealing about this product? ____________________

____

11. What do you find least appealing about this product? ____________________

____

12. Would you change anything about this product to make it more appealing or useful? ____________________________________

____

Part III — About yourself

13. Do you ever order products through:

(Check all that apply)

❑ Direct mail solicitations ❑ Catalogues

❑ Magazine ads ❑ Newspaper ads

14. What magazines do you regularly read? Please list them.

____

15. What is your employment?

❑ Professional (attorney, doctor, CPA, etc.)

❑ Managerial ❑ Technical/engineering ❑ Service

❑ Sales ❑ Arts ❑ Homemaker

❑ Other (please specify) ____________________________________

SAMPLE 6 — Continued

16. What is your age group?

❑ 18 –30 ❑ 31– 40 ❑ 41–50 ❑ 51– 65 ❑ Over 65

17. What is your household income?

❑ Under $10,000
❑ $10,001–20,000
❑ $20,001–30,000
❑ $30,001–40,000
❑ $40,001–50,000
❑ $50,001–75,000
❑ $75,001–100,000
❑ Over $100,001

Thank you for your response. The following information is optional but would be helpful to my study:

Name ____

Address ____

City ________________ State or Province _______ Zip or Postal code __________

LM/ ________________

Chapter 10

ANALYZING AND INTERPRETING YOUR DATA

Now that you've administered your survey, you need to analyze the data and determine what it means. This involves four steps:

(a) Examining and possibly editing the completed forms

(b) Tallying the responses

(c) Charting the responses to each question

(d) Determining the meaning of the responses

> *According to some views of evolution, complex life forms depend for their existence on a capacity to extract energy out of entropy — to recycle waste into structured order.*
>
> MIHALY CSIKSZENTMIHALYI,
>
> *The Psychology of Optimal Experience*

EXAMINING AND EDITING THE COMPLETED FORMS

Your first step is to go through all the completed questionnaires and make sure the responses are useful. In some cases, you may actually edit the responses, for instance, when you know what a respondent intended to say, but the wording or handwriting makes it unclear. In other cases, you will need to discard some responses or even entire forms. For instance, if (on a multiple-choice question) someone checked several boxes when the instructions said to check only one, you would have to discard that answer. There is no way to decide which of the three or four answers is the most appropriate. One bad response doesn't invalidate the entire questionnaire; just discard the improperly answered question and continue. You only need to discard the entire form when it's clear that the respondent misunderstood or deliberately disregarded most of the instructions.

TALLYING THE RESPONSES

Next, you need to gather all the questionnaires and record every response to every question. You can do this by hand or by computer.

By hand

If your survey was brief and administered only to a small sample (say, a 10-question survey given to 100 people), you can probably just stack the forms and go through them by hand. On a separate sheet of paper (your tally sheet), record each response to each question, then add the totals. The tally sheet might look like Sample 7.

If respondents added specific comments under the "Other" category, you could write those comments on a separate sheet, or list them below the tallied responses.

By computer

You can record data in your spreadsheet program, or a small amount of data can even be entered into a word processing program that has a simple calculating function. Once you've entered the data by keyboard or scanner, the program will then tally the responses for you.

But if your survey was more complex (for instance, if you administered a 50-question form to 1,000 people), you may find it useful to record and chart your data using a specialized survey application.

There are a number of computer programs designed to tally and analyze survey results. Computer programs can even help you design and select question-types for your survey. These include SurveyPro by Apian Software, SumQuest Survey by SumQuest, Market Reader Pro by Market Reader Pro, and NIPO Interview System by NIPO Software.

For small businesses the best of these may be SurveyPro. While not as powerful as some other programs, SurveyPro can tally as many as 2,000 questionnaires with up to 150 questions per form, handling two-choice, multiple-choice, ranking, and open-ended responses. The program will analyze your data and create charts. It also accepts data imported from Lotus 1-2-3. SurveyPro sells for around $1,195 (US) and, best of all, it's easy to learn and use.

Don't forget to enter your survey keys into your database. Your survey analysis program can cross-check the codes with other data and give you such potentially valuable information as the following:

SAMPLE 7
TALLY SHEET

QUESTION 1: HAVE YOU EVER SHOPPED AT NADINES?

YES

𝍸 𝍸 𝍸 𝍸 𝍸 𝍸 𝍸 𝍸 𝍸 𝍸

𝍸 𝍸 𝍸 𝍸 |||

NO

𝍸 𝍸 𝍸 𝍸 𝍸 ||

TOTAL YES: 73

TOTAL NO: 27

TOTAL: 100

QUESTION 2: WHAT DID YOU LIKE BEST ABOUT SHOPPING THERE?

Price 𝍸 𝍸 𝍸 |||

Selection 𝍸 𝍸 𝍸 𝍸 𝍸 𝍸 𝍸 ||||

Location 𝍸 |||

Atmosphere |||

Service |||

Other ||

TOTAL PRICE: 18

TOTAL SELECTION: 39

TOTAL LOCATION: 8

TOTAL ATMOSPHERE: 3

TOTAL SERVICE: 3

TOTAL OTHER: 2

TOTAL: 73

(a) Whether one mailing list drew a more positive response than another

(b) Whether respondents at Mall A answered significantly differently than those at Mall B

(c) Whether one interviewer's data was out of line (suggesting either dishonesty or influence on the part of the interviewer)

CHARTING THE RESPONSES TO EACH QUESTION

Once you've tallied the responses in each category, you should chart or graph the results. Charting serves several purposes. First, as the ancient saying declares, a picture is worth a thousand words.

For example, which is easier to understand?

This tally:

PRICE:	18
SELECTION:	39
LOCATION:	8
ATMOSPHERE:	3
SERVICE:	3
OTHER:	2

OR

This bar graph:

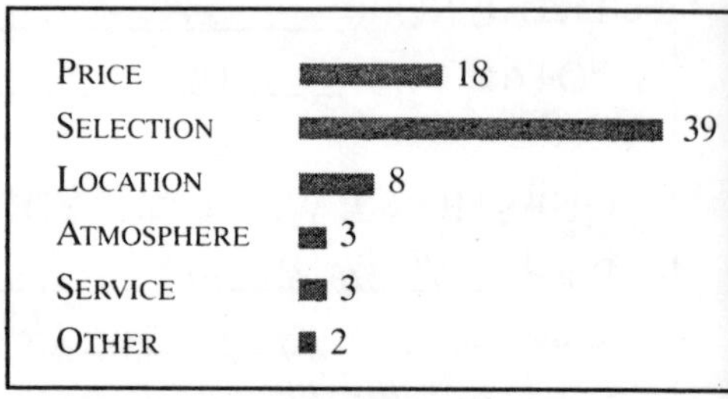

Charting makes it easier to read and interpret your data. It not only makes it easier for you, it makes it easier for bankers or venture capitalists who may be loaning you money based in part on your data. It makes it easier for managers or salespeople who need to work with the data. It makes it easier for customers to whom you may show the data. (Try using a pie chart to illustrate survey data on you and your competitors under the headline: *The facts show: shoppers rate our quality #1 over all the rest!*)

For many purposes, a simple bar diagram like the one above is the most readable and versatile method of charting, but other useful charting styles exist: a curve can be useful for charting responses to a ranking question; a pie chart can make a professional-looking presentation of multiple choice data and can help you see the percentage of people responding, rather than merely the relative numbers of people responding.

There are a number of methods for charting your data. If you don't have a computer, you can draw some simple graphs by hand. But that's a boring task and it's easy to make mistakes. If you've tallied results by hand, you can still use a computer graphics program to draw charts, entering the data into the graphics program by keyboard. (Be careful to enter it correctly, though.)

If you've tallied results with a spreadsheet or word processor, you can use that program's graphing function (if it has one) or import the data into a separate graphics program.

But it's when you use a specialized survey program like SurveyPro that you can really get the most mileage from charting. Among other things, these programs are usually designed to cross-check responses on your survey. If you gathered data on the age, gender, income, occupation, or education level of your respondents, for example, the program can cross-reference that data with other questions on the survey to yield much more detailed and sophisticated results.

Here's an example of the kind of results a survey program can give you that would be very difficult and tedious to get by other methods. A market researcher asked this question:

- What is the number one reason you chose our product? (Check only one)

  ❑ Price

  ❑ Appearance

  ❑ Service

  ❑ Durability

  ❑ Warranty

  ❑ Selection

  ❑ Other ______________________________

She made a bar graph of the overall response, as shown in Graph (a) in Sample 8. Clearly, price and durability are the two factors most influencing the purchasers of her product. However, when her survey application broke the results down by the respondents' gender, she got a much more telling result, shown as Graph (b) in Sample 8.

Based on these results, it's no longer accurate to say price and durability are the two factors most influencing purchasers. Clearly, price is overwhelmingly the biggest factor influencing most men, while durability is more important to women.

Taking it one step further, however, the marketer decided to see how men and women with incomes above $75,000 viewed price and durability. Those results are shown as Graph (c) in Sample 8. Here, the picture changes once again. In the high-income brackets, the interests of men and women merge, making durability clearly the number-one factor to a marketer interested in a high-income target.

SAMPLE 8
COMPUTER BREAKDOWN OF SURVEY RESULTS

(a)

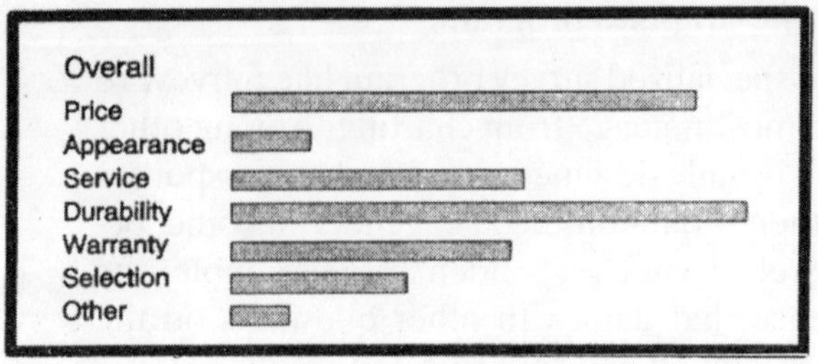

(b)

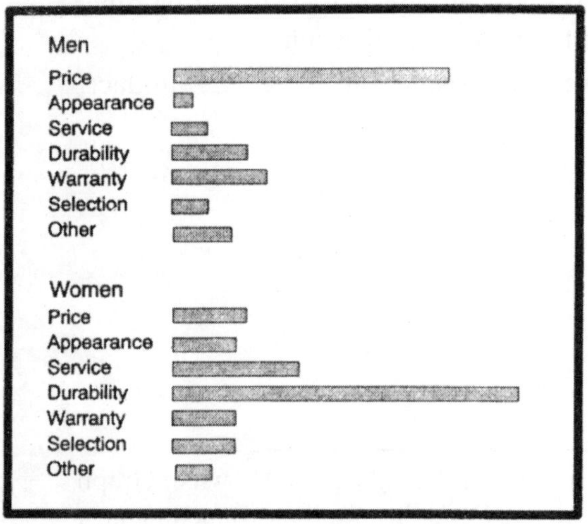

(c)

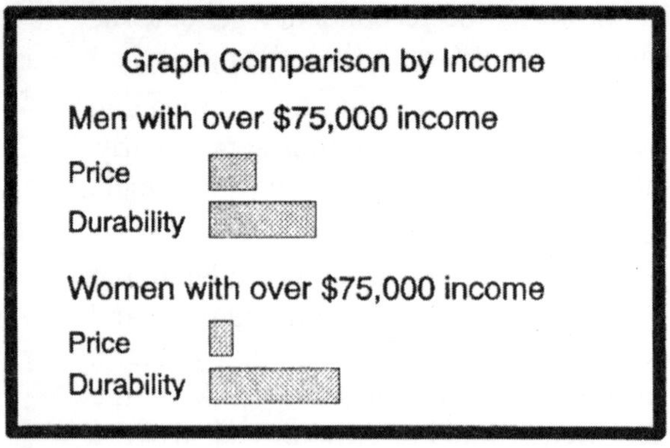

DETERMINING THE MEANING OF THE RESPONSES

To find the meaning in your carefully charted responses, look for the following four things:

(a) Trends

(b) Similarities

(c) Contradictions

(d) Odd groupings

The first two are signposts that can keep you on the right road. The second two are warnings that you may have missed a turn or that you risk heading full speed into a dead end.

Time to consult a pro? Professional market researchers are experienced at interpreting data. They can tell you when an apparent trend or contradiction is statistically meaningful and when it may merely be the result of a survey error. If you have any questions about the meaning of major points on your questionnaire, show a pro.

Trends

A trend, in this case, simply means a significantly high or low response to a given option. A trend might be that —

(a) 75 percent of women respondents named service as their most important consideration,

(b) three out of five men surveyed said they watch at least five hours of TV a day,

(c) 85 percent of respondents said they had heard of Bob's Sports Bar, or

(d) 67 percent of teenage girls surveyed said puce was the hottest new fashion color.

Trends will leap out at you as soon as you put your data into the form of a bar, a pie, or a curve, and can become more apparent as you break down data by different demographic groups. Trends can help you target your product or service to the strongest demographic group. They can also point to ways you can modify your offering to make it more appealing to that group.

Similarities

Similarities are trends shared by widely varying demographic groups. If your survey reveals that teenagers and middle-aged people, yuppies and blue-collar workers, all rate your product very highly, you know you have something that transcends age and income levels. But before you launch your marketing effort, go back and make sure you didn't get such a broad approval rating by asking leading questions, which would compromise all those favorable responses.

Contradictions

Contradictions can tell you a lot about your product. For example, let's say you administered a questionnaire to 100 people who used your new hand tool, the Micro Frammis, asking them to rate its ease of use.

Your results present a contradiction. Overwhelmingly, people find it easy to use. However, 25 percent of your respondents are telling you the thing is almost impossible to use. You need to find out why.

In this case, there's a clue right in the answer and the product. The Micro Frammis is a hand tool, and about 25 percent of the population is left-handed. Is it possible that the Micro Frammis is only a right-handed tool? Once you've established that this is the reason for the contradiction (and you may have to go back to some of your respondents to do that), you need to decide what to do about it. Can you afford to produce and market a left-handed model as well?

Contradictions can also point to flaws in your survey methodology. If people give answers which don't mesh (for instance, they say they would buy the product, then give overwhelmingly negative ratings), your questions may not have been clear enough.

Another reason for apparent contradictions can be the makeup of the survey sample. If the Micro Frammis were a computer game, for instance, you might get contradictory results if you included people of widely varying ages in your survey. In general, people over a certain age will tell you any computer game is difficult, whereas people under a certain age find most computer games easy to understand. This is when a specialized survey program comes in handy. You can break down the results by various groups and discover if one group is responsible for the apparent contradiction.

Odd groupings

Are you getting results you just didn't anticipate and can't explain? You need to track them to their source. For instance, a multi-state survey reveals that your new bottled soft drink is five times more popular with young boys in Hawaii than with boys in other states. Why? Are Hawaiian tastes different? Before you throw all your marketing efforts into the 50th state, you do some investigating and learn that bottle-cap collecting is the latest childhood mania in Hawaii and that your colorful cap is the major reason for the boys' interest.

Maybe you want to go ahead with a marketing push in Hawaii anyway. But armed with an understanding of the reason for your product's popularity, you can be better prepared to market effectively.

IF YOU FIND THINGS YOU CAN'T INTERPRET

What do you do if you can't track those contradictions or inconsistencies to their source? Or if your data seems in any other way incomplete or inconclusive?

> *I have spread my dreams under your feet; tread softly because you tread upon my dreams.*
>
> W.B. YEATS

It's possible (and for a first-time researcher, it's common) to discover that your survey didn't ask the right questions, or that your sample was incomplete or unbalanced. It's also possible that you asked great questions and screened your sample wisely only to discover some very mixed or inconclusive views in the market.

In that case, bite the bullet and take your survey and results to a market research professional. The professional can help you interpret confusing data. If the data is confusing because the survey was conducted incorrectly, the professional can help you compose replacement questions, then you can return to the field and do a partial resurvey.

On the other hand, if the majority of your data pointed you in a clear direction, and only one or two questions yielded odd results, you could proceed with your marketing plans, as long as those questions do not cover critical decision areas.

CHECK YOUR HYPOTHESIS

Once you're confident of the meaning of your data, go back and revisit the hypothesis you recorded on Worksheet 5. Have you proved it? Great. Proved a modified version of it? Great. Disproved it? Then it's time to decide whether you should proceed on your project with a revised hypothesis or abandon the marketing project and look for one that stands a better chance of success.

Case Study

Clarice Rogers uncovered a wealth of interesting data with her survey. She surveyed 225 women on 3 separate occasions at upscale shopping malls. Of the 225, 91 (or approximately 40 percent) said they owned address books or executive day planners.

About half of these (47) said they had purchased the product for themselves and the rest received theirs as a gift. As Clarice expected, Christmas was the biggest gift-giving occasion, with 30 people (68 percent of all gift recipients) having received their book then.

About 68 percent (153) of all the women surveyed said they would buy the *Calligraphy Book of Days*, with 58 percent (89) of those saying they would buy the book for themselves, 77 percent (118) saying they'd buy it as a gift for a woman, and just 7 percent (11) saying they'd buy it as a gift for a man. The totals in this question exceed 100 percent because respondents were allowed to make more than one choice.

On average, respondents said they'd be willing to pay about $29 for the book. Some said they'd give as little as $15, while others claimed they'd pay as much as $79. The $29 figure was disappointing; it would not be enough to guarantee a profit. But when Clarice cross-referenced the respondents' income with the price they were willing to pay for her book, she found that the higher-income women — her true target market — were willing to pay, on average, $43. Further cross-referencing told her that most of the potential higher-priced buyers were in professional and managerial jobs.

The single group that listed the highest average price ($57) was women working in the arts. But before deciding to market to this group, Clarice checked two other pieces of information. First, she cross-referenced them by income and discovered they were among the lowest in the survey sample; they might be moved to buy the book by their sense of aesthetics, but as a practical matter, might not be able to do so. Second, Clarice checked the total number of women in the "arts" category. There were only 17, a percentage and a survey sample too small to base a marketing strategy on.

Clarice found that fewer than 25 percent (56) of the total survey group owned any of the luxury art and office products she'd included for comparison. But cross-referencing once again, she learned that, among those women owning appointment books or day planners, 47 (or 51 percent) owned such luxury products.

Despite the fact that she conducted her interviews in a mall, she was pleased to discover that a substantial number of her subjects said they purchased goods through direct-marketing methods (mail, magazine response ads, catalogues). This answered a big question for her. Since she'd already established that she'd need to market outside her immediate area, she now felt confident she could do so via direct marketing, rather than the more difficult route of trying to place her product in retail stores.

Finally, while many respondents offered comments about what made the book appealing (the beautiful writing, the book's elegant, elongated shape, the generous spaces for writing appointments), even those who said they wouldn't buy the book found little fault with it. She would not need to go back into product development.

Her conclusions: Her best marketing method would be to use ads in upscale magazines and/or mailings to lists of upscale executive women, to price the product at $39.95, and to position it as an office tool for the woman who values style as well as success.

Chapter 11

WHEN YOU NEED TO HIRE A PROFESSIONAL

DECIDING WHEN YOU NEED A PRO

You can successfully conduct much of your own market research, but there are very definitely times when, if you can possibly afford it, you should hire a market research professional.

As we've pointed out, a professional can augment your do-it-yourself project in a number of ways, helping you to —

(a) identify your target audience and your survey sample makeup,

(b) compose or evaluate the questions on your survey,

(c) analyze and interpret the statistics you generate, and

(d) make sales and other projections based on your data.

There are also times when you might benefit by turning your entire research project over to the pros. In addition to their expertise, the pros can also offer you —

(a) interviewer training and monitoring,

(b) computer programs capable of processing tens of thousands of questionnaires,

(c) focus group facilities with hidden video cameras and two-way mirrors,

(d) phone interview facilities with dozens of lines,

(e) computer-assisted phone interviewing techniques,

(f) graphic design expertise for preparing questionnaires and reports, and

(g) statistical analysis skills.

How do you know what course is best for you? Take a look at these two situations:

(a) You are the middle-aged owner of a manufacturing business, considering adding a new product line that could mean a profit of thousands of dollars each month. Bringing out this new product line will cost you a hundred thousand dollars, most of which you will have to finance. If the product is a failure, your current profit may not cover the loan payments.

(b) You are a young adult with an "okay" job, but you want to open your own business to have more control over your own life. You've found a new use for an existing product. You can buy the product cheaply with no minimum order. For a few hundred dollars, you can be in business selling the product in your spare time. If it doesn't sell, you lose very little. If it does you can quit your job, hire a sales force, and run a successful business.

Both entrepreneurs will benefit from market research, but at what cost? The manufacturer ought to be willing and able to spend $5,000 to $10,000 or more to investigate the market potential of a new line. The aspiring entrepreneur would blanch just hearing such figures. However, this person could benefit by spending a day and a few dollars searching for market information.

The manufacturer risks everything by doing inadequate research. The young entrepreneur risks nothing more than a few hours trying to make sales.

Your business is probably somewhere in between these two situations, and you are the only one who can determine how much to budget for your project and how much of your own time to spend on it. You can spend nothing beyond a few dimes for the copies you make at the library, you can spend a few hundred dollars consulting with a pro at key stages of your own research, or you can make the major commitment to have your research conducted professionally.

When considering the value of market research to your business, ask yourself:

(a) How much do I have to spend?

(b) What is the benefit of research? What will I gain if it is done and done well?

(c) What is at risk? Jobs? Dollars? Reputation? My future?

(d) How much can I realistically do myself?

(e) What can a market research professional accomplish that I cannot?

WHAT PROFESSIONAL SERVICES COST

In general, market research firms bid by the project, basing their charges on hourly rates ranging from $75 to $250. Some may use a graduated fee scale, with lower rates for less skilled services, like data entry and telephone interviewing, and higher rates for strategic services like research design and analysis and focus-group recruitment. They will also charge for materials and other outside expenses.

If you are considering having a research firm conduct all, or a large part of your project, call several firms, explain your needs, and ask the firms to give you bids. Meet with them in person, if you can. There's usually no charge for the initial consultation, and the face-to-face meeting gives you an excellent opportunity to evaluate the company.

When preparing their bids, many companies routinely break their charges down into categories such as:

Professional fees:

- Research design
- Questionnaire design
- Focus group recruitment
- Data collection
- Programming/data processing
- Data analysis
- Report preparation and presentation

Material/supply fees:

- Phone charges
- Facility rental
- Printing of survey forms
- Shipping/postage
- Travel/per diem

TABLE 3
RESEARCH SERVICES COSTS

Telephone survey (including design and analysis)	$2,500 to $7,500
In-person survey (including design and analysis)	$3,000 to $10,000
Focus group (including facility use, participant recruitment, participant payments, moderator fee, planning session, discussion guide, analysis and report)	$1,500 to $2,500
Research design only	$750 and up
Questionnaire design only	$350 and up
Data collection only*	$1,000 and up
Programming/data processing only*	$500 and up
Data analysis only*	$500 and up
Report preparation and presentation*	$350 and up
Hourly consulting fees	$75 to $250

*Many reputable firms are not willing to collect, process, analyze, or report on data unless they have been involved in designing the survey. They are reluctant to take responsibility for potentially faulty or amateur methodology.

If you are in doubt about whether you can afford full-scale professional services, be sure to ask for this kind of breakdown. Then, if you decide to hire the pros only for limited services, you'll have a pretty good idea of the cost. Table 3 shows some typical costs for comprehensive research services.

You might also want to make use of the services of a strategic planning consultant, an expert who can take the results of your research (either professional or do-it-yourself) and help you put them to work. A planner will help you create your business or action plan, and can work with you on retainer for several months as you put the plan into action. Such an expert might charge $2,500 or more for the initial brainstorming/planning sessions, then $500 to $750 a month to help you implement your plan. You'll find strategic planners under "Marketing Consultants" or "Consultants" in the Yellow Pages. Or better yet, ask around your business network.

These fees will vary greatly from company to company, market to market, and situation to situation. Use our figures as a guide, but get accurate prices from research firms before setting your budget.

WORKING PRODUCTIVELY WITH A PROFESSIONAL

One way to find a market research firm or consultant is to look under "Market Research and Analysis" in the Yellow Pages. You can also talk to others in business and ask whether they have had any market research done, if so, who did it, and whether they were pleased with the work done.

When you visit with a marketing research consultant, provide him or her with as much information as possible, including —

(a) background information on your company,

(b) why you need research,

(c) all possible details about your new product or service,

(d) what kind of marketing plans you have, and

(e) the range of your budget.

Be prepared to hear techno-statistical jargon like descriptive statistics, chi square, T-test, Z-test, analysis of variance, multiple regression, and correlation. These are all statistical methods for analysis of survey data. Don't be intimidated if you don't understand. You don't need to. (After all, it's for this kind of expertise that you're going to a researcher rather than doing it yourself.) A market research consultant will be able to explain how these methods affect your survey.

From the beginning, agree upon the kind of relationship you and the research firm want to have. Do you want to turn everything over to the experts and just wait for the results? Do you want to be consulted at key stages? Do you actually want hands-on involvement with the process? Do you want the firm to show you its processes and define its terms step-by-step? Or do you not care to know? Define such terms at the beginning and you'll have less friction as your research progresses.

Case Study

When she really got down to serious financial and sales projection, Clarice found she was stumped. She finally took her data to a market-research professional and paid him to help her project sales and revenues. Unfortunately, he informed her that her survey sample, while excellent for a community-based marketing effort, lacked a broad enough base to allow her to make an accurate, nationwide sales projection. Still, he is able to help her make rough projections, warning her the projections contain large margins of error. Clarice knows she can't afford the time or the money to conduct a second, more accurate survey. So, based on the strong positive responses she got from the three executive women who tried her product and answered her in-depth questions, she decides to proceed.

Chapter 12

EVERYBODY OUGHT TO HAVE A PLAN

If success is a journey, your plan is the map, compass, guiding star, and vehicle for your trip. Before leaving home you should know the answers to these questions:

- Where are you going?
- How are you going to get there?
- Will you be driving straight through?
- Will you be stopping along the way?
- What happens if you run out of gas?
- Does it matter if you go by the back roads or the freeways?
- How will you know when you've arrived?
- What if you don't like it there?
- Is there really any there there?
- Do you really want to go?

Every market research project should result in an action plan that will serve as a road map to the marketing of your product, service, or company based on your research.

Every business, however small, should also have a business plan that spells out the company's goals, mission, vision, market positioning, management structure, and overall strategy for achieving success.

The action plan assures that you stay on the marketing path your research guided you onto. Your business plan assures that you don't lose sight of your long-term destination. Both types of plans can be an effective tool for raising money. To bankers and venture capitalists, a written plan says you've done your homework, assessed the risks, and are a careful planner. A written plan also helps assure that you, your partners, your managers, and your employees will all adopt the same tactics and goals for your business.

A large company may have one business plan and any number of action plans for marketing various products or services. Since this book is intended for very small or start-up businesses, this chapter will show you how to create a multipurpose action and business plan in one.

An important note: If yours is more than a one-person business, all your key people should contribute to the creation of your plan, and all your employees should be familiar with the plan and the philosophy and strategy behind it. The plan is useless if everyone isn't following it and if key people don't believe in it.

THE ELEMENTS OF YOUR PLAN

Here are some of the elements a typical business/action plan will contain:

(a) Four guiding statements
- (i) Mission statement
- (ii) Objective/goal statement
- (iii) Vision statement
- (iv) Positioning statement

(b) Corporate descriptions
- (i) Management/job descriptions
- (ii) Product/service descriptions

(c) Market analysis and marketing strategy
- (i) The market; its strengths and risks
- (ii) Strategy for reaching the market

(d) Finances
- (i) Start-up requirements
- (ii) Funding sources
- (iii) Projections

(e) Plan of action
- (i) Action timetable
- (ii) Worst-/best-case scenarios

Try roughing out a business/action plan before you have completed your research. This preliminary plan will give you direction and reflect your gut feeling about what you can achieve. Be sure to include alternate plans; you don't want to fall in love with one plan, then later find out it won't work. Just as you rechecked and revised your hypothesis to fit the facts, alter your plan to reflect what you've learned during your research.

> *Why not spend some time in determining what is worthwhile ... then go after that?*
>
> WILLIAM ROSS

> Susan Michaels, a television personality in Washington, saw a market for renting women's formal wear. She worked on her business plan for 18 months, doing a detailed analysis of the local market for formal wear by interviewing corporate event planners, cruise directors, and convention attendees. She analyzed her findings and figured she could make a profit by the time she rented a dress the second time. In the end, with her plan in hand, she was able to secure financing for A Grand Affair, her successful business venture.
>
> *Inc.*, March, 1992

FOUR GUIDING STATEMENTS

Whatever else it contains, your plan should open with several brief, comprehensive statements that define your company and state what you want it to accomplish.

Your mission statement

Your mission statement should state *simply* what your business does. It should define the broad purpose of your business, specify your chief product or service, and identify the market for the product or service. Although *mission* is a rather grand-sounding word, this isn't the place to make a high-flown statement of philosophy. Keep it simple and factual. The following are some typical mission statements:

(a) We are in the business of manufacturing quality boots for hunters.

(b) We supply paper products to users of office copiers.

(c) We offer professional house cleaning services for working women.

(d) We offer middle-income people a one-stop source for insurance and securities.

An effective mission statement should have these characteristics:

(a) It clearly identifies the business you are in

(b) It identifies the product or service you provide

(c) It briefly identifies your target market

(d) It is clearly understandable to all members of your organization

(e) It took some thought to figure out

Your goal statement

> *Our plans miscarry because they have no aim.*
>
> SENECA

You probably already have a broad understanding of the goals you need to achieve. If yours is a one- or two-person company, perhaps your goal is nothing more than to make enough money to live comfortably. If your company is larger or already established, you will have more elaborate and carefully thought-out goals.

Goals fulfill needs. Ask yourself some questions about your needs. What must my company achieve before I will consider it a success? What do I need to accomplish to satisfy my aims? The answer to these questions will give you your goal statement.

Here are some typical statements:

(a) We want to be among the top ten security companies in Canada by the year 2007.

(b) Our aim is to gross $1,000,000 in sales after three years of operations.

(c) We plan to become the largest-volume floral supply in Tulsa.

(d) My goal is to be selling my line of clothing to Nordstrom's Department Stores within two years.

Your market research can help you determine whether your goals are realistic. If you discover that they are not, you can step back and revise them in light of your new learnings.

Goal statements are as varied as the companies that compose them. But they often address one or more of these categories:

(a) Sales

(b) Productivity

(c) Market share

(d) Cash flow

(e) Profit

(f) Competitiveness

The vision statement

The vision statement is somewhat like the goal statement. But where your goal statement deals with "hard" information like profit and productivity, the vision statement talks "softly," about image, empowerment, community involvement, quality, and environmental concerns.

Instead of asking, What do we need?, you now ask questions like, What kind of company do we want to be? How do we want our community to view us? How should we treat our employees?

The questions will vary from company to company, and the answers will vary even more. Some companies will have vision statements closely tied with their corporate goals:

(a) By the year 2008 we would like to have every hunter in North America view our boots as the ultimate in hunting wear.

(b) We want to be seen as the hippest manufacturer of computer games for kids.

Others will be more outward-looking:

(a) We want to become a top-quality manufacturer of lampshades while providing jobs and advancement opportunities to the Hispanic community.

(b) We will be known as a company that sincerely values the lives of marine mammals.

> *Nothing is more terrible than activity without insight.*
>
> THOMAS CARLYLE

While your vision statement is a kind of "wish list," it should contain only those items you are realistically striving to achieve. If you trumpet your concern for clean rivers while secretly dumping toxic waste into the nearest stream, you won't be fooling anybody for long. If you pledge yourself to the highest service standards while cutting corners at every turn, your vision statement will become an object of derision to customers and employees, having the opposite effect from what you intended.

The positioning statement

Last, but certainly not least, among the four major statements comes your positioning statement. This is a single sentence which contains the answers to these three questions:

(a) Who is my best target customer?

(b) What is my company's (or my product's) competitive category?

(c) What is the chief benefit my target gets from my product or service?

> Positioning statements change as the market demands. A survey revealed that an irate public was fed up with credit information abuses. Equifax Inc. of Georgia responded by changing a portion of their positioning statement to "... the company most responsive to consumer concerns." Positioning is more than mere words: Equifax backed up its statement with a new customer-service phone center and 500 customer-service representatives.

For example:

- For hunters and outdoorsmen who care about top-quality equipment, Orion hunting boots deliver lasting reliability.

Notice how this statement identifies the target customer (hunters and outdoorsmen), the category in which you compete (high-end hunting boots), and the benefit (reliability).

Your positioning statement is vital. It is more closely tied to your marketing activities than any of the other statements. Every marketing and advertising decision you make should be based on it.

Your positioning statement is different from the other statements in that it identifies the target as specifically as possible and identifies the number-one reason you think those specific people should buy from you (e.g., not because you make boots for hunters, but because your hunting boots are reliable). It also deals specifically with your product, rather than your company as a whole. You should never do any advertising, marketing, public relations without asking yourself, Does this support my positioning?

CORPORATE DESCRIPTIONS

The next section of your plan should contain some basic organizational information. The information you include in this section will be particularly useful to employees and potential backers encountering your company for the first time. All this information can fall under two general headings:

(a) Management/job descriptions

(b) Product/service descriptions

Management/job descriptions

Under this heading list such information as the following:

(a) What type of organization are we (sole proprietorship, partnership, corporation, etc.)?

(b) What is our management structure (board of directors, president, CEO, COO, department heads, etc.)?

(c) What are the duties of each officer and/or department head?

In this section, you may also want to include a flow chart, if your organization is that complex, and brief resumes of your key executives. Don't try to pad it; if you are the only key executive (or even the only employee) don't feel the need to try to make it look otherwise. But describe yourself, your duties, and your background in a positive, businesslike manner.

Product/service descriptions

This heading gives you the opportunity to elaborate on the brief message in your mission statement. What more do you want to say about your product or service? About the benefits it offers? About the audience it is intended for, the market niche it fills? Do you sell other products or offer other services besides the one your research focused on? Do you do other things related to your main business? (For example, do you service the goods you sell?) Detail them here.

Don't write an essay, though. As with most other categories in your business/action plan, a paragraph or two, a page at most, is probably sufficient. But think about the banker, customer, or new employee who may see this information; what would you want them to know?

MARKET ANALYSIS AND MARKETING STRATEGY

This is the area in which you will make the most extensive use of your research results. This is also likely to be the longest section of your plan.

The market: Its strengths and risks

Under this heading use your market analysis research to identify things such as —

(a) the geographical area you serve,

(b) current customers — demographics and psychographics,

(c) potential customers — demographics and psychographics,

(d) the competition — who they are and what their strengths and weaknesses are, and

(e) risk factors.

Risk factors might include things such as —

- high unemployment,
- changing market conditions,
- unfair competition,
- high potential for new competition,
- proposed or existing government regulation,
- local businesses closing,
- uncertainties about your product (revealed by your primary research), or
- anything that could affect the market for your product.

> *Test results should always be interpreted in the light of ever-changing marketplace conditions.*
>
> Thomas M. Bodenberg
>
> *The Journal of Advertising Research,*
>
> October/November, 1990

If your survey or your secondary data revealed any weak or troublesome factors, don't leave them out of your calculations or your plan. Lay them out on the table; if you don't, someone else might — and ruin your presentation to backers or prospects. Consider going back and resurveying to answer any nagging questions before they become problems. But in the meantime, put them down.

Strategy for reaching the market

In this section include the following information:

(a) The pricing of your product or service and your reasons for setting that price point

(b) An overview of your proposed marketing strategy

(c) An overview of your advertising and promotion plans

(d) An overview of how you will use public relations to augment your advertising and increase recognition of your product/service

(e) A brief listing of key business relationships: suppliers, distributors, accountants, lawyers, perhaps even key clients

(f) Distribution methods

(g) Risk factors

Risk factors in a marketing strategy might include things such as —

- a distribution network prone to backlogs or breakdowns,
- changing supply prices,
- rising media prices,
- potential negative publicity,
- uncertainty about the proper price point for your product or service,
- lack of available shelf space for a retail product,
- a limited advertising budget, or
- anything that could affect your ability to successfully get your message or your product to your target market.

FINANCES

For many small businesses, this will be the most challenging section of the plan, both intellectually and emotionally. It's very difficult to make financial plans, particularly when dealing with the many unknowns a business start-up or new product/service introduction entails. Basically, your financial plan will cover three areas:

(a) Start-up requirements

(b) Funding sources

(c) Projections

Start-up requirements

This applies whether you are starting a new business or merely extending your product or service line. How much cash will you need to —

(a) develop your product or service,

(b) lease a building,

(c) furnish an office,

(d) buy or lease office equipment and supplies,

(e) print business forms,

(f) plan and conduct your initial ad campaign,

(g) hire employees,

(h) purchase insurance, and

(i) cover your first two years of operation?

List as many start-up costs as you can think of, even minor ones like office coffee service. It's better to err on the side of caution than to get caught even a little bit short. In the final draft of the plan, you can group some of these small expenses under Miscellaneous, but you should list them for your own benefit and so that you can respond if asked to account for them.

Funding sources

Time to consult a pro? Professional market researchers or business consultants may be able to make financial projections or sales projections more accurately than you can. Consider spending a few hundred dollars to get expert advice here.

Now, where will you get this money? From a bank? From family? From your own savings account? From venture capitalists? From partners or stockholders? From government or other grants? If you must give up some ownership or control of the business to get a particular type of financing, how much will you have to give and on what terms? In this section list the following:

(a) All planned sources of funds

(b) The percentage of your total funding each source will provide

(c) The terms of the funding

(d) Alternate sources of funding

Since you will probably be using the plan as a tool for dealing with bankers, you may not have all this information until later. In that case, list your known sources and terms, such as your own cash or a loan from your brother, then discuss the rest of your funding needs in more general terms. Explain what you need, where you hope to get it, and how you plan to pay it back. Listing your known sources will help increase your credibility with lenders (assuming the sources you list seem legitimate and do not impoverish you or obligate you to impossibly high payments.)

Projections

In this section include these items:

(a) Your projected monthly, quarterly, or annual budget

(b) Cash-flow projections based on expected sales

(c) An analysis of your break-even date

(d) A projection of your five-year earnings potential

These projections should be based on your most likely scenario (see **Action Plan** section below). Yes, there is a certain element of witchcraft to making projections, and rarely do projections turn out to be completely accurate. But by making them, you are showing investors (and yourself!) that you are looking ahead, doing your homework, and being realistic about your potential.

You should update this section of your plan soon after you see how your product or service is actually performing in the market.

ACTION PLAN

The contents of your action plan will be affected by many factors, including how well established your business is, what kind of funding you need, and how slowly or rapidly you expect the market to adapt to your product. In general, however, you should include at least two categories: an action timetable and worst-/best-case scenarios.

Action timetable

In this section, lay out a step-by-step timetable, including target dates, for such activities as —

(a) contacting bankers or potential backers,

(b) getting financing approved,

(c) signing contracts with distributors (if any),

(d) placing ads or conducting promotion,

(e) introducing the product or service to the market,

(f) doing follow-up surveys,

(g) reviewing success of product or plan, and

(h) making any needed adjustments to the product, packaging, or marketing methods.

Worst-/best-case scenarios

You should actually develop three plans of action based on your survey data:

(a) Worst case

(b) Best case

(c) Most likely case

Worst case

Using the most negative reading of your survey and secondary data, forecast a scenario for the worst marketing conditions you might encounter. Project what might happen if the least number of prospects made a purchase, if a pending economic downturn actually happened, if an important customer went out of business. Try, as best you can, to decide the probability of this worst case actually occurring.

You don't have to be ridiculous about it; there's no need to forecast what might happen in event of nuclear war or an invasion from outer space. But do include every negative factor your data says you are likely to encounter. Don't exaggerate, but don't fudge and don't kid yourself.

Now, ask yourself if your product, service, or business could survive the worst case. Then make a plan to help you cope in case the worst really happens.

Best case

Now, with the most positive data from your survey and your day at the library, forecast a scenario for the best marketing conditions you might encounter. Project what might happen if the maximum number of prospects made a purchase, if the economy turned upward, if a new major customer came into town. Do your best to calculate the odds of the best case occurring.

Once again, stay within the realm of the likely. Don't forecast what might happen if Michael Jackson endorsed your product (unless the "Gloved One" has already expressed an interest!). But do let yourself get realistically rosy.

Now ask how you would do in the best case and make a plan to help you take advantage of it. Remember that the best case can be a mixed blessing: if sales are that strong, will you have trouble filling orders, or will your customer-service staff be so overtaxed they'll drive customers away?

Most likely

Now determine what is most likely to happen and write a scenario for that. Establish ways of moving from this plan to the best- or worst-case plan in the event market conditions change. Spend some extra time on this plan to make sure you've taken everything into consideration.

BUSINESS PLAN ASSISTANCE

Obviously, many parts of the plan, especially those calling for projections, are difficult. There are, however, plenty of resources to help you prepare your business/action plan:

(a) Your business network

(b) Books, videos, and other training materials

(c) Consultants

(d) Computer programs

A company that is not a direct competitor may be willing to share all or part of its plans with you, and your local library or bookstore will carry guides to writing a business plan. For more information, see *Preparing a Successful Business Plan*, another title in the Self-Counsel Series.

Consider requesting assistance from the Small Business Administration (United States), the Service Corps of Retired Executives (SCORE) (United States), or the Business Development Bank of Canada (BDC). Locate them by looking in the phone book or by contacting your local chamber of commerce. You can also try calling the business school of a local college or university, which will have experts on its staff. As we have mentioned, market-research professionals can advise you on making forecasts based on data.

One of the easiest ways to write your business plan is with a computer program designed for that use. These programs ask you questions in a logical sequence. You fill in the blanks, then when the program is done, you can print out your plan in a professional-looking format. Some programs even come with a sample completed plan to guide you. While a computer program cannot help make your projections more accurate, it can help organize your thoughts and assure that you don't forget vital elements.

You'll find business plan software at your local software store or advertised in computer or business magazines. You might look into: Biz Plan Builder (about $150) or FisCal (about $100). When you use FisCal with Halcyon's Current RMA Industry Standard's Data Disk ($150), you can compare your company with the industry norm. Another program, Success, Inc. (about $130), uses a question and answer dialogue. Most of these programs require that you have additional word processing and spreadsheet software.

One of the dangers of amateur and customer research is that a nonrepresentative sample will be drawn, ultimately leading to the wrong conclusions. A second danger is that, even if a representative sample is used, the amateur market researcher will not be versed in the … statistics needed to search for complexities.

WILLIAM L. SHANKLIN IN *SIX TIMELESS MARKETING BLUNDERS*

USES FOR YOUR BUSINESS/ACTION PLAN

The primary uses for your business/action plan are, as we have discussed, to serve as —

(a) a road map for you and your employees, and

(b) a tool to help you get financing or other backing.

Consider other uses for your plan including —

(a) sharing it with advertising or marketing firms, and

(b) sharing it with suppliers, customers, or prospects.

Sharing it with advertising or marketing firms

Every aspect of your advertising, marketing, public relations, and promotion should reflect the mission, goals, vision, and positioning stated in your plan. The most efficient way to do this is to put the plan into the hands of the people in charge of those activities. Instruct them to consult your plan whenever they select media, brainstorm creative directions, write copy, do photography, write news releases, or do anything on your behalf.

Since much of the information in the plan is highly sensitive, have these outside agencies sign an agreement to keep the information confidential.

Sharing it with suppliers, customers, or prospects

Want to get an important supplier on your side? Want to persuade a big prospect to take a risk and deal with your new little company? Want to show an existing customer you're serious about giving him or her excellent, long-term service? Try showing them sections of your business plan.

There are many ways you can do this, depending on the nature of your business and the relationships you have with customers and suppliers. The simplest way to share part of your business plan is to post your mission and vision statements where customers can see them. You can also quote parts of the plan in brochures, sales letters, and other company literature. When romancing large clients or responding to requests for proposals, you can include large sections of the plan in specially prepared proposals.

Of course, you won't want to show the entire plan to suppliers or customers. Some of the information is too confidential. But show them selected portions that demonstrate your sense of purpose, the

Four major reasons why loans are turned down and where market research can help you improve your chances:

(a) The business idea was too risky

(b) The business plan was poor

(c) The purpose of the loan was not acceptable

(d) The character, bearing, and personality of the individual asking for the loan was not appealing (research will improve your knowledge and confidence)

results of your research, and your knowledge of your field. They'll be impressed.

PRESENTING YOUR PLAN

Experience is a good teacher, but she sends in terrific bills.

MINNA ANTRIM

When presenting your plan to VIPs, including bankers, backers, and members of your board, make sure your presentation is as strong as your documentation. To do this, you don't need to be a brilliant public speaker. You don't even need to be calm (great presenters are often as nervous as newcomers). You just need to be prepared. Try these steps:

(a) Make sure your plan is attractively laid out, with charts and graphs to clearly display numeric relationships, readable type, and simple but attractive binding. Consider "extras," like using color, having the report polished by a professional writer, or producing it on a desktop publishing program.

(b) Consider in advance whether your presentation would benefit from the use of flip charts, overhead projections, video, or other visual aids. If your presentation is nothing more than sitting across a desk from your banker, you probably won't need these devices. If you must stand before a group, visual aids will help you make your points and keep everyone's attention.

(c) Prepare an outline of your most important points. Include information such as what your product/service is and why you believe it will be successful, why you conducted your market research, the methods you used, what the key results were, your sales and profitability projections, your own background and qualifications, and why you believe this is a good investment.

(d) Concentrate on making a strong, knowledgeable presentation. Your audience will remember your presence more than your words. When they later want to recall your facts and figures, they can look in their copy of your report.

(e) Use short sentences and everyday language; don't try to impress anyone with market-research terminology or professional jargon.

(f) Draw the audience in; address individuals by name, look them in the eye, ask them questions, and encourage them to respond to your individual points.

(g) Keep it brief. Your presentation should never go over an hour.

YOUR BUSINESS PLAN REVISITED

Once you've done your research and completed your plan you will use the plan constantly. Even if you put it on the shelf and rarely look at it, you will still be guided by the information it contains.

But a plan is never really done. At least once a year, you should take it off the shelf and carefully review it. Are you still moving toward that goal? Are you fulfilling your vision? Has your customer base changed? Has the economy caused you to readjust financial projections? As business and the world changes, you will want to adjust your plan. (This is where you'll especially appreciate the flexibility of a computer program.)

Any time you make major changes in your business, you should rewrite your plan and, of course, back it with additional research. If you introduce a new product or service, open a new company or new division, or enter a new market, it's time to update the research and update your all-important plan.

Case Study

Clarice Rogers produced a 10-page business/action plan using her personal computer and an inexpensive desktop publishing program.

She found it easy to write her mission, goal, and vision statements, but agonized over her positioning statement, knowing how much impact it would have on her entire marketing approach. She finally came up with this:

> For executive women, the *Calligraphy Book of Days* is the appointment scheduler that brings a sense of style and elegance to their busy routine of appointments.

While very simply phrased, her positioning statement conveys several important marketing decisions. First, Clarice has decided to aim her message directly at executives, deliberately excluding social users from her marketing. While she knows many social users will certainly buy her product regardless, she doesn't want to risk "muddying" her advertising message or her marketing plans by trying to aim at two quite different audiences at once.

Second, she has decided to think of her competitive category as being appointment schedulers rather than appointment books. This is her acknowledgment that executive women don't necessarily decide to buy an appointment book. Rather, they seek the most attractive or convenient method of scheduling. By making that simple word switch, from book to scheduler, she is mentally placing her product in competition with calendars, computer programs, and other methods, as well as other appointment books. She is also broadening the potential market.

Some other key points of Clarice's plan were the following:

(a) Based on the small number of executive women in her region, and the fact that her product is compact, light, and durable enough to be easily sent anywhere, she has identified her target market as being executive women nationwide.

(b) Her initial marketing effort, therefore, will be to rent a portion of the mailing list of a noted working-women's magazine and to reach these members of her target with a direct mailing including a full-color brochure and sales letter. Since mailing lists can usually be purchased broken down into various categories, she initially decides to order a list containing the highest income subscribers in a five-state area. She will expand the geographical area if the initial mailing generates sufficient sales.

(c) She decides to start her marketing push in October, the opening of the holiday buying season and the time of year people begin thinking of purchasing new calendars.

(d) Her largest risk factor, she believes, is the high price of her product relative to other appointment books and calendars. But she believes she can overcome this by marketing her book as a luxury item — a work of art as well as a business necessity.

(e) She identifies her key business relationships as being with her printer, her book bindery, and an as-yet unnamed banker. Because her product is so specialized and so elegant, only a handful of printers and binderies will be competent to produce it; therefore one of Clarice's goals is to establish relationships with these suppliers in which they feel almost as much ownership and pride in the product as she does.

(f) Initially, she will distribute the book herself, with the help of hired temps, as individual orders arrive. She will ship by UPS, using her home office as the mailing center. She determines that this method of distribution will serve her in both her worst-case and most likely scenarios, but that she and her temps will be overwhelmed if her best-case scenario occurs. She contacts an order-fulfillment house (whose address she found in a trade association directory during her day at the library) to learn whether they could handle distribution efficiently. This becomes her backup distribution source.

(g) She estimates start-up costs to be $39,000. Since she will operate out of her home and continue to be basically a one-person business (assisted only by temps) for the foreseeable future, and since she won't immediately rely on this business to make a living, she has relatively few major needs. The bulk of her start-up money is allocated to product printing and binding, brochure copy and design, brochure printing, list rental, and postage. She has $10,000 of her own, and a commitment for another $10,000 from a family member, which would not have to be paid back.

Armed with bound copies of her plan, she schedules appointments to make her presentation to three local bankers. She hopes to get a bank loan for 75 percent of her start-up capital needs, but is prepared to put up 50 percent of the cash herself if she meets too much resistance from the bankers.

Chapter 13
THE BEGINNING

Where your initial market research ends, everything else begins. You are now prepared to finance, produce, and market your offering and, we hope, be successful at it.

> *Never let the future disturb you. You will meet it, if you have to, with the same weapons of reason which today arm you against the present.*
>
> MARCUS AURELIUS

But remember that just because you put this book on the shelf, it doesn't mean you should put market research on the shelf. In one form or another, research should become part of your continuing business activity. Keep clipping statistical articles from trade magazines. Keep writing customer comments in your "Us" file. Take the time to prepare brief five- or six-question surveys to slip into billing envelopes, present at your counter, or give to clients in your waiting room. Look, listen, and learn. Then file everything for future reference.

Some day, as you prepare to introduce another product or service, as new competition threatens your markets, or as your company expands into new cities, states, or provinces, you will want to conduct formal research again. Then you will find that those files of data have turned into pure gold that will help you identify trends, set research directions, and save money and time.

When you reach the point when you can afford to turn future market research entirely over to professionals, your experience and your alertness to market conditions will help you give better direction to the pros and better understand the results they produce.

Congratulations for getting this far. Market research can be daunting and discouraging. As one businessman commented, "I hate market research. Nine times out of ten it tells me I shouldn't do what I want to do." But obviously even this man believes in market research or there wouldn't be any nine times out of ten! Even when it turns you away from your plans, market research can lead you to much better ones. We wish you the best in all your business endeavors, and hope this book will continue to serve as a resource as you continue down the road to success.

Case Study

Clarice Rogers went to the appointment with the first banker pumped up with nervous energy, but confident of her plans. The banker commented on the quality of her proposal but, noting the uncertainty of her sales projections, turned her down flat. "Too risky," was the verdict. "Nobody's going to pay that kind of money for an appointment book."

The second banker seemed interested. Then he asked her to bring her husband "because I'm sure he knows more about the financial details." Clarice bit back a stinging response and left. Even a good plan and a great presentation can't always overcome prejudices.

The third banker listened intently, then called a colleague to hear the remainder of Clarice's proposal. They congratulated her on the excellence of her work, and even though they, too, noticed her somewhat uncertain sales projections, one of them said to her, "Anyone who'd do her homework this well has what it takes to run a successful business."

On the spot, they gave her a tentative commitment for 67 percent of her needed capital, and offered to establish a generous credit line if she could show positive results from her first mailing. On a handshake and a cloud, Clarice Rogers left to begin her marketing venture.

Chapter 14

ACCESSING MARKET RESEARCH DATA

USING COMPUTERS TO GATHER INFORMATION

In the previous chapters, we showed you inexpensive ways to gather research information and data. We have only briefly mentioned the use of computers and the Internet in your office and in the library. Sometimes, computers can be intimidating, but if you are willing to spend a little time and add a few dollars to your budget, the computer can offer volumes of both primary and secondary data as well as other information. The computer can be an effective tool for you to use in your market research projects.

> *With a computer and a sense of adventure, you may travel the world.*
>
> A PROVERB REWORKED BY DON DOMAN, JR.

If you are already familiar with computers and have your own up-to-date computer system, you may use your computer skills to your market research advantage. If you are buying a computer in the near future, we recommend that you purchase one adequately equipped. Explain to the salesperson how you will be using the computer. Also, if you will be using an online seıvice, check its equipment requirements for service. We suggest a CD-ROM or CD/DVD reader, a good printer, and a modem, or cable, or DSL high-speed connection.

> *What do computers do on Saturday nights? They go on datas, of course.*
>
> ANN BISHOP

With a computer, not only can you run general business programs and market research survey and analysis programs, you can also access databases, bulletin boards, and forums. If you are not comfortable using computers, you can still receive the benefits of computer research by hiring someone else to retrieve the research information.

DATABASES YOU CAN OWN OR ACCESS FOR A FEE

One way to get up-to-date market knowledge in the midst of ever-changing market conditions and an ever-growing information explosion is to consult databases containing information that can help your business. You got a taste of using databases during your day at the library and the databases there will probably be sufficient for your initial market research. But if you want data coming into your own business or home, or for ongoing research, there are three ways to acquire it:

(a) Subscribe to online services

(b) Purchase CD-ROMs and DVDs for your computer

(c) Consult marketing information companies

Online services

Online services are electronic databases that you access via telephone and computer modem. There are hundreds of services that give you access to thousands of separate databases. Some are very specialized, offering medical research data, social trends, stock market and investment information, and so on. Others are much more general.

Information is updated at least daily and in some cases several times a day on most online services that carry newspapers and wire service data.

In addition to their basic subscription fees, online services charge for their data in one or more ways:

(a) Connect time

(b) Flat fee per search

(c) Fee per search

(d) Flat fee per week or month

Connect-time pricing means you pay for the amount of time you are connected to the database. As computers and modems have increased in speed, shortening the connect time, companies have begun to add print and display charges to their connect fees. These are called variable-rate charges, and they make it a bit difficult for you to budget for data searches.

Flat fee per search usually requires you to buy a number of passwords, paying a fixed fee for each. Each time you conduct a search, you use one of the passwords, which then self-destructs and becomes invalid.

Fee per search means you are charged for each search, but instead of a flat, predetermined fee, the charge is based on a sliding scale, usually depending on the number of searches you make.

Flat fee per month or week is ideal if you will be using the service frequently. You pay one flat fee for a given period of time and don't have to worry about the number of searches you conduct or the amount of time you are connected to the system.

There are more online services becoming available every day. To find the best ones for you watch for their ads in publications like *American Demographics, Inc., The Wall Street Journal, The Financial Post,* magazines for computer users, and specialized trade publications. Appendix 2 lists a few popular online services.

Some online services offer electronic bulletin boards and forums (with very select subjects) where you can ask questions or make comments to other subscribers on a particular subject. For instance, you might connect with a forum on public relations and marketing, then ask questions about survey techniques. People from around the country and the world will respond with opinions, knowledge, and advice.

CD-ROMs/DVDs

CD/ROMS and DVDs are available from many sources, including your local software store, high-tech or specialty catalogues, and a few of the same firms that offer online data services. They may carry some of the same data offered on line, and some of the same data you found in reference books at the library, where it was free. But if you have frequent need for certain limited types of data, a CD or DVD may be a cost-effective tool for you. CD-ROM disks cost anywhere from about $100 to more than $1,000.

As a general rule, when you may need access to many different types of data, subscribe to an online service. When you have extensive need for one or two types of data, purchase disks.

Marketing information companies

Basically, marketing information companies use the same online or CD-ROM/DVD databases you can access yourself, then sell information to you. There are, however, advantages to using their services.

One advantage is that they subscribe to more services and search more databases than you could reasonably afford. So, while their services can be expensive (about the same hourly rate as market research firms plus additional charges for connect times or specific searches), they can be cost effective and great time savers.

In some cases, these firms also cross-reference the data, interpret it, report on it, and give you a more sophisticated level of information than you would be likely to get on your own.

Some firms specialize. One may gather data on particular segments of society, providing businesses with information on trends among teenagers, seniors, Hispanic-Americans, western Canadians, urban dwellers, suburbanites, etc. Another may specialize in patent or trademark searches. Yet another may track business trends and opportunities in Asia and the South Pacific.

Some firms offer a one-time service; you come to them, tell them what you need, and they put the information together for you. Others sell their information by subscription, offering weekly, monthly, or quarterly reports on markets, trends, scientific findings, etc.

While few small businesses can consistently afford the services of marketing information companies, they can be a valuable resource to call on when —

(a) you don't have computer equipment to access databases,

(b) you have a very specific need, such as a patent search, or

(c) you want interpretation and reporting as well as data.

You can find marketing information firms advertising in *American Demographics* magazine and listed in that publication's annual directory. The directory may be available in the reference section of your library. Some may also advertise in specialized trade and business publications.

Appendix 1
A SAMPLING OF SOURCE MATERIALS FOR MARKET RESEARCH

This appendix provides a taste of the many publications you can find at your library. Most of these references have data online as well as general publications. There are many more available that may be applicable to your particular research. Ask the reference librarian for assistance in your specific field.

UNITED STATES

AT&T Toll-Free 800 US Directory (Bridgewater: AT&T Communications Americas). A national directory of companies with 800 number service.

Brands and Their Company: A Gale Trade Names Directory (Detroit: Gale Research). A two-volume listing of 194,000 consumer-oriented trade names, brand names, design names, etc. This contains names only, not trademarked symbols and logos. But it can serve as a first resource when checking to see whether your proposed product or business name is available for use.

City and County Data Book (Washington: Bureau of the Census). A supplement to the *Statistical Abstract* which gives similar information on a more local level.

Facts on File (New York: Facts on File). A compendium of information from news sources.

Franchise Opportunities Handbook (Washington: US Department of

Commerce, Bureau of Industrial Economics). A guide to available franchise opportunities and instructions on setting up a successful franchise.

Gale Directory of Publications and Broadcast Media (Detroit: Gale Research). A three-volume guide to all print and broadcast media in North America.

Gale Encyclopedia of Associations (Detroit: Gale Research). Information on trade associations, many of which can supply you with data and information.

The Municipal Yellow Book (New York: Monitor Publishing). A guide to who's who in leading city and county governments.

The New York Times Index (New York: New York Times). A guide to articles that have appeared in *The New York Times*. Your library probably carries the *Times*, or has it available on microfilm.

Places Rated Almanac (Boyer, Rick and David Savageau. Chicago: Rand McNally). A frequently updated guide to all major US cities. Contains economic information, schools, cultural organizations, climate, water quality hazards, leading industries, crime rates (by type of crime), etc. A good reference when considering moving, relocating a business, or opening a branch operation in an unknown area.

The Readers' Guide to Periodical Literature (New York: H.W. Wilson). An index to all the articles that have appeared in hundreds of consumer and business magazines over many years. Many of the periodicals mentioned in the *Guide* are carried by your local library. Current issues are displayed on shelves; older issues may be stored in a back room or available on microfilm. Ask the librarian.

Small Business Sourcebook (Detroit: Gale Research). This book profiles more than 200 types of businesses. It gives information to help you get started, contact trade associations, and find suppliers.

Standard and Poor's Corporate Reports (New York: Standard and Poor's Corporation). A seven-volume bound set of booklets containing information about individual companies.

Standard and Poor's Credit Week (New York: Standard and Poor's Corporation) and *Value Line Ratings and Reports* (New York: Value Line). Bound booklets of current analysis of various companies, stocks, etc.

Standard Rate and Data Service (Skokie: Standard Rate and Data Service). A series of media directories listing names, locations, phone numbers, contact people, rates, and technical requirements of thousands of media. There are separate books for television, daily newspaper, weekly newspaper, consumer magazines, trade magazines, etc.

The Statistical Abstract of the United States (Washington: us Department of Commerce, Economics and Statistics Administration, Bureau of the Census). A compendium of various types of data about the United States. For example: consumer price indexes by major groups over the last 30 years; most popular recreational activities over the last 20 years; the number of Hispanic public officials serving during the last 7 years; disbursement of highway funds by state for the last 10 years; and average number of days with precipitation — selected cities.

The Thomas Register (New York: Thomas Publishing). A 26-volume set of information on manufacturers, listed alphabetically by product or service category and by company profile; also contains pages from companies' product catalogues.

The US Government Manual (Washington: Office of the Federal Register, National Archives and Records Administration). An annual containing lists of government agencies including addresses, phone numbers, and contact names.

US Government Purchasing and Sales Directory (Washington: US Small Business Administration). A directory and instruction book for any small business wishing to purchase from or sell to the federal government.

US Industrial Outlook (Washington: US Department of Commerce, International Trade Administration). A manual containing business forecasts for 350 industries, complete with trend charts and analysis.

CANADA

Blue Book of Canadian Businesses (Toronto: Canadian Newspaper Services International). Similar to the *Who's Who*.

Canada's Postal Markets (Toronto: Maclean Hunter). Has statistics on consumer spending, vehicles driven and registered in given areas, data on citizens' mother tongues, etc., all organized according to postal codes.

Canadian Advertising Rates and Data (CARD) (Toronto: Maclean Hunter). A series of media directories listing names, locations, phone numbers, contact people, rates, and technical requirements for the majority of the advertising media in Canada.

Canadian Almanac and Directory (Toronto: Copp Clark). Similar to the *Corpus Almanac* but a little less government oriented.

Canadian Business Index (Toronto: Micromedia). A reference guide to Canadian periodicals and reports on business.

The Canadian Government Buyer. A directory and instruction book for any small business wishing to purchase from or sell to the federal government.

Canadian News Facts (Toronto: Marpep Publishing). A compendium of information from news sources.

Census data from Statistics Canada (Ottawa: Supply and Services Canada). This data comes in many forms including books of national statistics, books of provincial statistics, and books of statistics for individual cities. Information includes population characteristics, average number per family, average income, and population by gender and by age.

The Complete Direct Mail List Handbook (Burnett, Ed. Englewood Cliffs: Prentice-Hall, 1988). A guide to help make your direct mail campaigns a success (including your direct mail surveying).

Corpus Almanac and Canadian Sourcebook (Toronto: Corpus Information Services). Canadian researchers are fortunate to have this comprehensive guide that, in addition to standard almanac-type information, contains:

- addresses and phone numbers of Canadian magazine and book publishers
- associations and societies (more than 350 pages of listings)
- radio and TV stations
- federal, provincial, territorial, and selected municipal government agencies
- libraries: public, university, and private

This book can be invaluable in leading you to other sources of information.

The Directory of Directories (Detroit: Gale Research). This handy guide can lead you to other handy guides more specific to your interests. Want to know who belongs to a certain trade association or business group? *The Directory of Directories* can help you find out.

The Directory of Sources (Toronto: Barrie Zwicker). A paid listing of "experts" who can speak or consult on many topics.

Export Canada (Surrey, B.C.: CanExpo Publishers). Help for anyone interested in marketing abroad.

The Financial Post Canadian Markets (Toronto: Maclean Hunter). More information on the characteristics of Canadian cities and regions.

The Financial Post Survey of Industrials (Toronto: Financial Post Corporation Service Group). Information on the characteristics, health, and growth of various industries.

Market Research Handbook (Ottawa: Statistics Canada). Contains general demographic information of interest to market researchers.

The Patent Office Record (Ottawa: Supply and Services Canada). A weekly listing of patents issued in Canada.

Who's Who for business. There are a number of these (e.g., *Alberta Business Who's Who, Ontario Business Who's Who, Who's Who in Canadian Business*). These can help you discover the key contact people in your business world and learn something about their background.

OTHER

Japan Trade Directory (Tokyo: Japan External Trade Organization). Lists Japanese companies by specialty and in alphabetical order.

Made in Export (Frankfurt: Made in Europe Marketing Organisation). An English-language magazine published in Germany and containing information about European marketing opportunities.

Your Market in Japan (Tokyo: Japan External Trade Organization). A series of monthly newsletters broken down by industry type (e.g., packaging machinery, textile machinery).

PERIODICALS

You can get a lot of useful information from business publications such as —

- *Benefits Canada* (Toronto: Maclean Hunter)
- *The Canadian Business Review* (Ottawa: Conference Board of Canada)
- *The Financial Times of Canada* (Montreal: Financial Times of Canada)
- *The Globe and Mail Report on Business* (Toronto: Globe and Mail)
- *Small Business* (Toronto: Financial Post)
- *Western Commerce and Industry* (Winnipeg: Mercury Publications)

LOCAL AND REGIONAL RESOURCES

Most of the references listed above are national publications. You will also find statewide, provincial, regional, and local data useful. Try the following:

- Maps of the region and local cities
- Economic newsletters pertaining to the area; contains stock prices, earnings estimates, interest rates, economic trendlines, profiles of selected businesses, etc.
- Magazines published by the local chamber of commerce or Economic/Region Development Administration
- Lists of community and/or business services containing addresses, phone numbers, and contact names
- Real estate sales updates, published by local offices of major real estate companies, giving updated home, land, and commercial property prices for all areas within the city and county
- The consumer price index for the nearest metro area, covering the last 20 years
- Community profiles giving such data as per-capita income; per-capita retail sales; length of commutes; local media; population breakdown by age, ethnicity, and other factors; schools, utility costs, and so on
- Directories giving an overview of local transportation, educational opportunities, community services, etc.
- A copy of your region's overall economic development plan
- Booklets of facts and figures about the region
- Telephone books for local communities and major cities

Appendix 2
DATABASES

ONLINE SERVICES

You can find out almost anything on the Internet. Here are some search terms — keep your data needs in mind — to use for market research:

Business Database Plus
Business Dateline
Business Demographics
Canadian Company Information
Canadian Department of Commerce
Corporate Affiliations
Demographic Information Profiles
Earnings and Growth Estimates of Companies
Economic Estimates and Market Analysis
European Company Information
Global Sources
Globe and Mail
Information Canada
Information USA
Legal Research Center

Marketing/Management Research Center

New York Times

Patent Research Center

Public Relations and Marketing Forum

Researching a Company

Standard and Poor's

The Thomas Register

Trademark Research Center

US Department of Commerce

US Government Publications

Vista Environmental Profiles

Some of the online services you'll find offer free listings for your company. If you are not ready to submit your company, make a list of the Web sites for future entry. Take advantage of any free listings you find. If you have a Web site, an additional link may help your Web site place higher in search results. If you don't have a Web site, you may still receive business from a free listing.

Many of the online services also have their database information available on CD-ROM or DVD. Some of these can be expensive especially for a small business conducting market research. A quick visit to Office Depot or Amazon.com may fill your database needs with more affordable alternatives.